Friendship at the Farmers Market

With all the best,

Bich Nga Burrill

Bich Nga Burrill

Cover photo: Lynn Karlin

First published by Dog Ear Publishing
4010 W. 86th Street, Ste H
Indianapolis, IN 46268
www.dogearpublishing.net

ISBN: 978-145750-397-9

This book is printed on acid-free paper.

Printed in the United States of America

Table of Contents

Introduction and Special Thanks..1

The People...3

Notes from My Kitchen 5

The Essentials 6

A Spring Feast..10

Soup 12

Small Bites 17

Bird of All Seasons 29

From the Sea...46

For the Love of Pork..58

Tofu 77

Rice and Noodles...94

The Special of Everyday Vegetables 105

Salad for All Season..118

The Salt Factor in Rubs...134

Summer Fare..135

Sweet Treats...147

White People Food...158

Recipe Index 172

Story Index 175

Introduction and Special Thanks

It has been over four years since I started this project. I couldn't have done it without the help of my husband and Samantha, our youngest daughter. The time frame couldn't be more perfect, since a few loose ends received closure in a much unexpected way.

Since I started writing, I have more respect for the meaning of "Something was lost in translation" and at times, even the best effort attempted was failed to nail down what I wanted to express. I'm not a trained writer, but I have plunged into the process with sheer joy and passion and therefore I'd hope you can feel it in every page. If you already know me, then you'll know every word is mine. I wish to represent the book as if I was there talking to you, guiding you through all the recipes and telling you how every story begins and how it ends.

Last, but not least, please forgive me if any grammatical errors occurred. Enjoy the flaws since they are a part of my charm. When I first started cooking outside the home I was a caterer for private family functions, birthday celebrations, and graduations, etc. One day while participating in an outdoor event a man showed up at my table, bought an egg roll and before his last bite asked me to join his indoor market. I took his name and number, but I really didn't give it another thought.

Did he say a farmer's market? What did I know about cooking for people who came to certain place? I had never been to one. I went home looked at my schedule and cleared one Saturday afternoon. Then, I picked up the phone, called and told him I'd join his market for one day to satisfy my curiosity.

That one day of working a farmer's market turned into fifteen years, many more markets and I am still going strong. I took just a few entrées and some spring rolls, nothing fancy. I found myself having a good time chatting with people, customers as well as fellow vendors. On top of that all my food sold before the day was over and that was the beginning of a new chapter in my vocation. Now these many years later I regularly attend four to five markets a week with help from my husband, as our youngest daughter has graduated and has started a new chapter in her life. I have learned and grown much over the years, but for the most part I'm still in a learning process. I have to thank Rick

1

for getting me to my first market, Bob Bowen for talking me into doing Bar Harbor plus Stonington markets, Rose Fisher of Fisher Farm for the short but sweet Northeast Harbor, and also Caitlin from Appleton Creamery for encouraging me to join the Belfast market.

A special thank to Bob Whelan for his friendship, help and encouragement.

Bob Whelan is a good friend of mine, a five stars diamond from Orono Farmer's market. At the market, the two of us habitually communicated in Vietnamese and that's attracting attention from people around us. I hope that make my friend feel special because I do.

The People

All types of people come to farmers markets and I'd like to introduce a few:

The come-along
They're here because they get dragged in by a friend or member of family. There is a big fat chance we (the vendors) will never see them again, I can spot this type miles away. "Hey, I'm here but don't think for a red hot minute that I'll buy anything." They even avoid looking at a vendor's ware, fearful they might see something they want.

The happy one-timers
They happen on the market or tag along with a friend. The people who belong in this group usually ask questions and most likely will ask to taste some samples. Sometimes they make an attempt at small talk and may even buy something. I know they're being nice but what I say goes in one ear and out the other. We'll never see them again.

The free loaders
Every market has a few who belong in this category: singles, couples and quite often even whole families. They have no intention of buying anything. Their mission is to sample as much as they can, to spot the freebies. I once observed a man encouraging his kids to eat more, before he dragged them away from a goat cheese vendor to another food vendor.

The one- day stands
Heard of a one night stand? We have one day stands. In this group the people are so happy to be at this kind of market; so excited. He or she will buy everything in sight and then you'll never see them again.

The short, but sweet, affairs
They come steadily, buy generously, but only just long enough for us to notice them and then they disappear forever. Where do they go??

The long meaningful relationships

We don't see them often, but they always come back.

I'm blessed with a lot of customers of this type.

The precious gems

This is the main group, the backbone, the fuel that runs the Farmer's Market's engine. They come often, know what they want, and are knowledgeable about the products. We know their names and they know ours. We know their shopping habits and they appreciate that we remember. They always take time to talk on a personal level. They are our friends and they really care for our well being.

The five star diamonds

Each market has only a handful of these folks. They make time and work around their schedules so they can come to visit us. Not much will keep them away from the market.

If one has to go out of town, we'll know about it ahead of time. We see them like clockwork. They are loyal and faithful. Like the time one of my customers was absent one week. I asked, "I missed you, is everything alright?" The customer answered, "It was a terrible week I had to take my best friend to the hospital. While he was in the emergency room, even though I was worrying about him, I was also fretting about missing the Farmer's market."

The next generation

I enjoy watching the young children that come to the markets. Rarely does one see the usual kicking and screaming that happens elsewhere. The children visiting the Farmer Markets seem happy and willing to sample new foods. Many tell me about their week while eating a favorite market treat. On many occasions I wish I could capture these moments with a camera, because the images would make a wonderful poster for Maine's Farmer's Markets.

I'm blessed with a lot of kids who belong in this precious group. Trust me, they know what to expect out of chicken fingers and fried rice.

I participate in four/five markets a week in the summer. I'm often asked which my favorite is and I haven't an answer. Each market has a unique atmosphere and trademarks that make it the favorite when I'm there.

From Mother's Day weekend to mid November you will see me at the markets. Then I take a break to enjoy (endure) Maine's long and wonderful winter.

I have a lot to be thankful for at my Thanksgiving table.

This book is my way of thanking my faithful customers, those people who make time to come and visit me week after week.

Notes from My Kitchen

I'm blessed with a lot of customers and there's little doubt that with many there's a special friendship. However most are the pickiest eaters on the planet. They know how to cook and have sophisticated pallets. These people will not put up with ho hum foods.

They expect the tops in tastes and I always work hard to deliver the best that I can. Using fresh ingredients is the first step in allowing me to achieve the tastes I envision and wish to deliver. I don't mind working hard to deliver what they have come to accept, it's my privilege. It's the same way I approach this cook book. I hope you don't mind working just a little bit harder and being a little bit more adventurous with me and my second book.

Please, be daring and add a touch of your own to any dish. I will pave the way for you. Before we get to the fun part, I have a few words about ingredients. So, please take notice, because I'm not going to remind you and bore you to death with each recipe.

Note: Lower case "t" means teaspoon and upper case "T" means tablespoon.

The Essentials

Oil

If oil is not the single most important ingredient in cooking, then I don't know what is. Oil activates the spices, which deliver aroma. Oil also makes food feel smooth in your mouth, making it feel pleasant. Picking your every day cooking oil is important. I know people who use olive oil for everything. I know olive oil is healthy, but I don't use it every time I cook. If a recipe doesn't call for olive oil, don't use it. For the foods in this book, your every-day oil should be flavorless one such as vegetable, soy bean, canola, or corn oil. Peanut oil is excellent in stir-fry, but because of many people's food allergies I do not use it in the foods I prepare for the markets.

Salt

You don't have to spend big bucks on any kind of special salt. Use what you are comfortable with. However, look at the spice rubs located on chapter 12 for more information.

Sugar

Let's face it, if I only cooked with salt and pepper, I wouldn't be writing this book. I have been cooking for a long time and what a small amount of sugar can do to certain dishes will never cease to amaze me. Use a sugar substitute if you have an issue with sugar. I will not use sugar substitutes, unless a client asks for it, since I do not like the way they taste and believe me you deserve to eat food that tastes good!

Soy Sauce

Now, we're talking about seasoning. Soy sauce delivers to your taste buds the way salt alone just simply can't. I use light soy sauce for everyday use. At times, I also use dark soy sauce and/or mushroom soy sauce to enrich taste and appearance. Pick the brand you would like to use every day but use it carefully until you are familiar with its salt content. You can always add more, but you can't add less. It takes more time to fix a dish that is over seasoned and it hardly ever turns out right.

Fish Sauce

This seasoning is Vietnamese but it's certainly not my starting place for every dish. I only use it when I cook my ethnic dishes and Thai dishes. When I do use it I let people know. If the word "fish" frightens you remember that fish sauce doesn't have a strong fishy taste or smell in these recipes because we are using only enough to get an ethnic flavor.

Flavored Oil

I will tell you how I make flavored oil at the bottom of this page. This item is very important in my kitchen. If you don't want to bother with it, that's your choice. Just use plain oil however, if you want to turn heads, make the extra effort.

Oyster Sauce

This is indispensable when you need more depth in a dish. Invest in a high quality bottle of oyster sauce. It is worth every penny. There's also a vegetarian version available.

Wine

Designing a wine dish is like casting a play. While no wine could ever be the main character in cooking, it can be great in a supporting role. Even the simplest of wines have the power to lift a dish to the next level by its aroma. Rice wine or dry sherry are often used in this book. Mirin is a sweet wine which I use for braised dishes or as base for marinade. Though they are not wines, gin, brandy, and tequila are good with some dishes.

Sesame Oil

Another seasoning item I find indispensable in oriental cooking is sesame oil. I like the dark and thick version from Japan (They're the authorities on this subject.) A little goes a long way. If you don't use it often, store it in the refrigerator.

Broth

Last but not least, always use broth; the worst broth is still better than water. This is one item you should always have ready in the pantry (or in the freezer if it's homemade). If you don't want to take the time to make your own, you can stock up around the holidays because it is usually on sale at two or three cans for a dollar. However, being a food snob I have no choice but make my own. What else am I going to do with all the bones I have left over and all the herbs from my garden?

Every chef has her or his signature broth. What suits me might not be right for you. For instance, I seldom use celery; it has no taste yet can have a dominating aroma in broth. Then there is parsley, although it's a god send in Italian cooking, it doesn't work for me. I just can't hack its smell. This green herb always reminds me of the scent from a kind of flat bug that crawled all over my cousin's house in Vietnam. Thanks to my cousin whenever I'm not motivated to do my housekeeping chores, all I need to do is take a whiff of parsley.

Flavored Oils

Oil that's infused with herbs is often used and quite important in my cooking process. If you want to create your own signature tastes, this is one of the tools. The chore is simple and the sky's the limit. Keep on experimenting, I still do.

Use a wok or heavy gauge pan that's not aluminum and pay particular attention to the heat. High heat will make it burn before it has achieved the potential aroma. Heat that is too low will take forever. Who has the patience for that?

Vegetable oil, canola oil, corn oil or even peanut oil is suitable for the job. Have a bowl with a strainer ready because as soon as the herbs or spices start getting brown they will need to be lifted out of the hot oil immediately. From there, the oil can be cooled off, stored in a glass jar, and refrigerated.

Crispy Onion and Oil

This is made with shallots, my first choice, but sometimes shallots are expensive. Besides, depending on the onion you use, such as Vidalia, the fried onion is so good that I can't help but eat it before it even cools off. Choose a firm fresh onion. Slice it thin. Squeeze out the juice, but save it to use later in soups, meat loaf, stews, etc...

For every 2 cups of oil you'll need 3-4 cups of onion, let it boil rapidly then lower the heat. Stir occasionally. When you see the onion starting to get a bit brown at the edge, that's when you have to pay full attention to the project and stir constantly until they're golden brown. With a slotted spoon remove immediately and place in a strainer. Use the back of spoon to press down and spread out. This action will stop fried onion from further browning. What you'll have is a perfect batch of crispy onion that has many uses, plus aromatic oil. Store them separately. Both the crispy onions and the oil will last for months in the refrigerator.

Scallion Oil

2 cups of oil
4 cups scallions washed, and dried thoroughly, cut into 1-1/2 inch pieces.

Proceed as for crispy onion. This particular oil will keep for a week in the refrigerator.

Use it in sandwiches, rice salad, noodle, salad etc.

Crispy Garlic and Oil
2 cups oil
1/4 cup sesame oil
2 cups coarsely chopped garlic

Process as for onion oil, except after removing it from the oil, you may add dried hot pepper and pepper corn to the hot oil and let them stay there overnight to intensify the aroma. This oil has many uses, from stir-fry to salad, to marinade for the grill when you need a bit of spiciness with an edge.

Hot Peppers Oil
1/2 cup oil
1/4 cup sesame oil
1/3 cup of hot pepper flakes

Place peppers in a clean jar (a jar that can handle heat). In medium stainless pan, heat oil to hot stage. Pour hot oil into jar, stir well and let it cool.

Red, Hot and Beautiful Oil
Here is oil that will stand up for its name, I use it in Spanish dishes, Moroccan dishes and of course, that's only the beginning.

1/2 cup oil
3T annatto seed
2T pure red chili powder

Proceed as above

A Spring Feast

The robin's slam into the sunny window was lethal and it crashed to the ground. I picked it up, amused by the plumpness of its breast. I gave the situation a little thought before I cleaned it up, rubbed it with a touch of rice wine, salt, pepper, and five spices powder. Then I wrapped a curl of orange peel around a fresh clove of garlic, tucked it neatly inside the bird's cavity and for a final touch I inserted a tooth pick starting from the beak right through its upper back.

I heated the toaster oven to 350 degrees, sat it down on its legs and roasted it for 20 minutes.

I didn't need to check the timer, judging from the aroma. I knew when it was ready.

I removed the exotic feast from the oven, transferred it to a tiny platter, covered the tip of the tooth pick with a small red cherry tomato, and then garnished around it with a few sprigs of green herbs. As I took a step back and admired the art I just created my two harshest critics entered through the front door.

My daughter Samantha walked through the kitchen, made a dead stop at the sight of the display on the counter. Her bewildered eyes quickly met my coy face.

"No, you didn't", she cried.

My husband said almost immediately, "I'll take a piece of that!"

With tweezers in my left hand to stabilize the lower part of the drum stick, I used embroidery scissors to snip it off from the body and handed it to him.

"Samantha, you prefer the breast, right?"

She gave me a stare down and sneered,

"I'll pass, thanks," and sauntered off in keen disgust.

I said "This is your chance to say I've eaten wild Maine robin.

The man of the house chuckled,

"It's not bad!"

That really was high praise considering this was the first time I ever prepared wild fowl.

He ate two more pieces while Sam continued to be grossed out.

"As if you can do any better with window kill!" I laughed.

Tilly and Simon barked knowing that they would soon be feasting on succulent bird.

Tilly is a Yorker mixed with toy Poodle. She's a four and half pounder who has a deep obsession with food. She loves French bread with Pate and everything else I serve her. She possessed the "peel me a grape attitude" most of the time; she must have been a movie star in her former life!

Simon is a loveable seven pound Maltese. He's a rambunctious happy go lucky guy who loves being outside with his grandfather.

A couple years back, we were supposed to babysit them for just two months, while our oldest daughter Amanda, their mother, participated in the Ironman Arizona competition.

So with spring feasts like this, why would they want to leave? They didn't! The grand babies are happy Maine residents now.

Miss Tilly's favorite meal is usually fresh out of the oven roasted chicken. She'll settle for leftovers if I heated it up perfectly, otherwise, between chewing she definitely sends me a look that's says, "Grandma, you are a slacker today"

Simon is a boy, so, of course he likes his beef! Grilled flap steak marinated in a light ginger soy dressing would be his top pick; he'll settle for 90 percent lean ground sirloin only if I grill it to perfection, meaning no pink at all!

These pups may have originated in California but they're Mainers now.

Soups

THE PINK DIAMOND

She was one of my regular customers. For years, she came to visit me most every Saturday morning. Her hair neatly styled and the way she dressed was usually flawless. She said she does all that just for me. There was one particular pink outfit that's I really liked, so I told her if she doesn't know what to wear, go for that one. Then over time I noticed she wore more pink clothing. I sincerely expressed my appreciation toward her efforts.

Time is an unforgiving process but she was still very easy on the eyes. I remember teasing her, "I bet you turned a few heads in your day" to which she very quickly responded, "I still do!" Some of us would like to borrow that line (me included) but it wouldn't be an easy task to deliver the way she did.

Like clockwork, she'd show up around noon and most of the time if she remembered she'd bring her own containers. She liked everything that's hot and spicy, so the hot and sour soup is the one regular item she would not leave without. If she has to go away she would let me know. Then three weeks go by and I haven't seen her. The following week a man showed up and he introduced himself as the Pink Lady's son. He told me something that I had suspected; she was in the hospital. He said, "This thing she'd been battling for sometimes took a turn for the worse."

"I'm sorry!" I whispered.

"I think you know why I'm here," he weakly smiled.

"Yes sir I do." I packed the soup, wrapped it up neatly and handed it to him.

"Please tell her this one's on me and I hope to see her soon" I said, my voice cracked.

The following week I didn't see the pink lady, and when I saw her son he leaves without the soup.

Hot and Sour Soup
4 to 5 cups of stock or 2 cans of broth
8 ounces soft to medium tofu julienne cut
4 ounces mushroom, white button, shiitake or portabella sliced

3T rice or white vinegar
2 to 3T soy sauce (Depended on the stock)
1T fresh grated ginger
1 to 3 t hot pepper flake

Bring all the above ingredients to a boil, cover, and lower the heat to a simmer. Cook from three to five minutes for the mushrooms to release their flavors. Add 2T cornstarch mixed with 2T water stir well, swirl in 2 beaten eggs. Last but not least add 1- 2 t sesame oil and few drops of hot oil (optional).

A tea spoon of sugar maybe added to make peace with the sharpness of vinegar.

Egg Drop Soup

This is an easy and quick soup to make. All you need is the broth you already prepared on hand and of course eggs. Great for breakfast!

1 can of chicken broth or 2 cups homemade
2 beaten eggs
1T light soy sauce
1/2 t sesame oil
2T scallion, chopped (optional)

Bring broth to a boil, gradually add egg. Swirl around so the egg forms a silky thread, pour in soy sauce. Turn off heat, add sesame oil and scallion.

Asparagus with Crabmeat

I have a fond memory of this dish. Back before the catering business, one thing was quite clear; I knew I could cook however I really don't know much about business relationships. So when people invited me to participate in events around the Bangor area I would jump in without questioning all the details: that's unwise!

This particular time, we were taking part in a festival to celebrate cultures without the knowledge of what kind of crowd we were going to have and without any advertising.

We, the market members, showcased our different foods. It wasn't a good affair; the majority of the people were expecting stuff like French fries and hot dogs. Thank heaven the times have changed.

There I was, fully loaded with pork, egg plant and Thai basil, spring rolls, plus a big pot of asparagus soup with crab meat. Tagging along with me were my two girls, Amanda and Sara. We did sell some foods, but nobody touched the soup. So when Amanda was asking me for some of that green stuff I knew she just said it to make me feel good. With skeptical eyes, I watched as she sips the first spoon, she doesn't make face instead she smiled and said,

"This is really good Mom, don't worry I'll eat it."

She wasn't just saying that for my benefit because during the course of the whole day's event she ate most of it. Until this day, if a pot of this soup is on top of the stove when Amanda's around, she'll eat the most or all of it.

This is a Vietnamese classic!

This entire project takes less than five minutes.

4 cups homemade chicken broth or 2 cans of store bought
1 can asparagus or ½ lb fresh cut into 1 inch pieces
1/2 lb fresh crabmeat
4oz mushroom, julienne cut
1 beaten egg
2T soy sauce
Salt and pepper to taste
2T cornstarch or arrowroot starch mixed with 2T water and a dash of sesame oil

Bring broth to boil, drop in asparagus, when it starts boiling again add crab meat, swirl in egg and soy sauce, adjust with salt at this point, then gradually add the mixture of starch to thicken it up. Cook vegetables to the desired tenderness. Remove from heat before adding sesame oil.

The Power of a Sincere Thank You Note

When I was featured in the Boston Globe years ago I hoped it would help find a publisher for my first book.

It wasn't all futile in that attempt as a couple of publishers called but the format of my book didn't fit into the so-called mainstream cook book, so, no deals happened!

After reading my article in the Globe a gentleman from Quincy called with an interest in purchasing my book whenever it got in print.

For the next two years, he would call from time to time just to check if the book had been published.

Finally it happened and he got his books in February few years back. We were delighted to send one of the first copies. In return I got a beautiful, lovely thank you note from that gentleman. He praised my work and purchased several more for his friends. I was so touched, we sent out more books for him together with a thank you note of my own.

Every few months for several years I would get other letters from him saying things like,

"My friend used to serve in Vietnam, I think he can use a copy of your book, please send one to him."

"My friend's wife just passed away, he has to cook for himself, and he needs a copy of your book."

"My dear friend's having a surgery, she can use your book to entertain her while she stuck in the hospital, please send one to her."

"My friend has a cold; she can use the chicken soup recipe in your book."

He always included a check for a little more than necessary and his always delightful thank you note. I haven't spoken to him for a couple years and we've never met, but every time I see that little envelope with his name tacked up on the wall I can't help but have a smile in my face and a warm feeling in my heart.

Miso Soup with Tofu and Greens

Green vegetables, tofu and Miso; these three elements combine can easily deliver a good message to some people and turn others off. Speaking for myself, I just happened to like the taste of this soup and if there's benefit to my health in any way, then I consider it a good bonus. This is the kind of food that warms my heart, the way a sincere thank you note would do.

1 block of soft tofu, sliced into small ribbons
4 to 6 cups of green such as tatsoi or baby Bok Choy
1T crushed garlic
1T grated ginger
1/4 cup scallion cut into 1inch
3T soybean Miso
Hot pepper flake to your taste
6 to 8 cups of broth
*Up to 1/4 cup soy sauce (see note)
Dash of hot oil and sesame oil

In a medium soup pan with 1Table spoon of oil, sauté Miso with ginger, garlic, hot pepper flake and scallion until fragrant, pour in broth, and tofu.

Slowly proceed with soy sauce to your taste, adding the greens and bring it all to boil. Cook until greens are tender, but not mushy- 3 to 5 minutes. Remove from heat before adding sesame oil and hot oil, if use.

*Note: You have to be careful with the soy sauce because of the salt content in Miso.

Fiddle Heads

A Maine treasure! This green creates mixed feelings, either you love it or hate it. Because it grows wild anyone keeps their picking place a big secret much like a top fishing hole. I get mine mostly at the Farmer Market and sometimes from my man.

Hot and Sour Shrimp with Fiddle Head Soup
1lb of shrimp shelled, deveined.
4 cloves of garlic
2 hot peppers such as Serrano, Jalapeno or Thai dragon
1/2 t each of salt and ground black peppers
3T fish sauce
2T garlic oil

In the food processor pulse the above ingredients until it forms a paste, chill.

Have it ready:

1 pint of clean fiddlehead
5 to 6 cups of stock
3 to 4T white vinegar

Bring stock to a boil, put in greens, add shrimp paste by spoon in boiling stock and add vinegar. Adjust seasoning, a spoon of sugar might be added. You don't want to overcook the fiddleheads. Tender on the firm side is the way to go. No herbs are needed because you want to taste the natural wild and earthy fiddlehead. Freshly ground black pepper and that's all you need. Some of the older Mainers I know add butter.

Small Bites

For the Love of Dumplings

Names were changed in this story to protect the privacy of my customers.

Deena always has been my gemstone. We had known each other for quite some time before her marriage to Roger fell apart. Soon after they divorced Deena found her a new playmate. He's younger than her ex, has more hair and dresses a heck of lot better than Roger on any day.

One sunny, historic afternoon Roger returned to the market, smiling ear to ear as he introduced me to a newer version of Deena. Although she was thinner and not quite as "hippie" as my friend, she can easily be mistaken as Deena's younger sister. A couple of markets later Roger returned, alone.

(I stick my nose into everybody business, I see it as a part of my job, OK!) I asked him," Whatever happened to the smaller version of Deena?"

"Ah, we didn't get along" Roger said, he sounded depressed.

"Lighten up, sometimes bad things happen for a good reason" There was my two cents worth of comfort.

It doesn't take long before Roger showed up with another Deena look alike except she was much rounder.

I was speechless and kept my mouth shut (It's a rare occasion) Poor Roger! It took him all that time to figure out that he liked meat on his bones.

This is one case I know I can analyze; I could be wrong but I doubt it. I think when it comes to searching for what we want, women are better at it.

Now you'll probably think "What's all that have to do with a cook book?"

Well there's a happy ending to this story. Deena's still in bliss with new man, Roger's still in the hunt for his latest Deena. The thin Deena's back with a much younger opposite version of Roger, and they all happily belong to my dumpling's club so instead of only the two I now have five or six buying.

Happy Dumplings

Unless you like the task of mixing and rolling homemade dough I see nothing wrong with using the commercial pre-prepared brands you can find at any grocery store these days. They are thinner and if you don't use them all up just wrap and freeze for later use. In this recipe; you'll need approximately 28-30 wrappers.

Making the wrappers
2 cups all purpose flour
1/2t salt
2/3-1 cup boiling water
Extra flour (for dusting)

Make a well in the center of flour, gently mixed in hot water and salt; knead until smooth and elastic. Cover and let it rest for at least 1/2 an hour.

Divide dough into thirty equal balls, flatten each ball with your palm and with a rolling pin roll them into flat circles approximately 31/2 to 4 inches across. Cover the pastry to prevent it from drying out.

Filling
1/2lb of ground pork
1/2 lb of chicken breast, coarsely chopped
4 ounces of shrimp minced
 1/2t salt and 1/2t pepper
2T oyster sauce
1T cornstarch
1T rice wine, dry sherry or brandy
1egg white
1t of sugar
2t of garlic oil or sesame oil
1/2 cup shiitake mushroom coarsely chopped
1/4 cup scallion coarsely chopped

In a large mixing bowl blend all the above ingredients. Depending on how plump you like your dumplings put about 2t to1T of filling into each pastry. Wrap the excess dough around the meat. Squeeze lightly just before you get to the top so a bit of filling oozes over like a mushroom. Lay dumplings over a greased steamer rack leaving a space in between each. Steam over high heat for 15-20 minutes, serve with dipping sauce.

Dipping Sauce
1/4 cup chicken stock
2T light soy sauce
1T rice vinegar
2t sugar
2t sesame oil and a dash of hot oil

Tip: Dry Shiitake mushrooms should be soaked at least for 1/2 an hour before use so plan accordingly. An easy way to cut off the stem is to use the tip of scissors.

Save the broth from the soaking and the stems for stock.

Dumpling with Tofu and Spinach

This is a hot item on my table at any market. I successfully am selling it to the people who can't stand to say the word tofu, much less consume it.

1lb of soft tofu, drain and blotch dry with paper towel
10oz baby spinach, blanched, squeezed out excess water
1T dried egg white
1T potatoes or corn starch
2T dried mushroom powder*
2T soy sauce
2t sesame oil
Salt and pepper to taste
1package of wonton wrapper or dumpling wrapper**

In a medium bowl, crush tofu and mixed it well with the rest of ingredients.

Put approximately a tablespoon full in each wrapper. You can fold around it and form like an open face dumpling, also known as Siu Mai. You can also make a pleat on top with one side, then press it against the smooth side and seal them together. For this folding version, you can set it on top of a skillet with a thin layer of oil and brown the bottom. Pour in a cup water or broth, put on a lid. Bring it all to boil, lower the heat, and cook for five minutes. This is how you make pot luck dumpling.

To save calories dumplings can be set in steamer and cooked for ten minutes.

This recipe makes approximately 3 dozen dumplings.

*Dried mushrooms can be pulsed in a spice grinder or a clean coffee grinder. This step will help to eliminate the moisture from tofu and spinach which helps toward the forming process.

**The wonton pastry is thinner and is much harder to use compared to the homemade one so take notice.

Sister Tien

She was my friend in the past before Lily entered the picture. She was the oldest daughter of my mother's best friend who I wrote about in my first book: the one with an alcoholic husband.

When Tien turned nineteen, she fell in love with a boy next door whose family was a rival of hers in the silk trades. She became pregnant and because she loved the boy she told her father that they were going to get married. He, in a drunken frenzy, began beating her before she was able to tell him she was four months pregnant. He beat her so badly she had a miscarriage and almost bled to death. She was never able to have children.

Soon as she could walk she ran away from not only her family, her first love, but me too. She went to Saigon, about forty miles away, and starting a brand new life. I was so sad; she was not only like the older sister I never had but she was also my best friend.

I'm not so sure what she was doing for work those years we were out of touch. I looked her up when I left home. She didn't say much and I didn't press although I was curious how she could afford a high end condo and surround herself with actors, actresses and musicians.

That's how my connection with show biz got started. It didn't take very long for me to realize I was in a very wrong business. It turned out I couldn't act nor could I remember lines. The only things I had going for me were my age, my semi decent body and the belief that I know everything about the business!

So now after forty plus years I can still visualize the scene in her condo the first evening I visited. The room was filled with smoke plus the scent of perfume and Crown Royal.

She was having a party!

Though the room was full of people she spotted me and quickly greeted me at the door.

"Well, well, little sis, your timing is perfect! What brings you to this side of town?"

"The aroma of food of course if you can get through the smell of cigarette and booze," I said as we gave each other a hug. She lowered her voice saying,

"It's kind of sad when people think they have to smoke and drink to have good time"

"I can see a lot of people in here. What kind of party is it? "I asked.

She whispered in my ear, "The kind that pulls money out of people's pockets. We're doing a fund raiser for a new television show"

The 'we' she implied must be her boy friend, but I did not know exactly what he was doing at that time. Now looking back, I see he fit the description of a producer or maybe a talent agent. I was looking at my faded blue jean and tank top with hesitation, "Maybe I should go, I don't fit in."

"Don't be silly! Go to my room and change into a lacy blouse, that's all you need to do."

I changed my tank top for a blouse but I also helped myself to a pair of stiletto heels. Empowered by the silky red blouse and the matching lip stick, I was flying high and walking like I was on my fourth drink.

On a huge table there were massive amounts of food: crispy rice puff with shrimp, roasted quail, pork Char Siu, and salted chicken. I was in heaven with all that food and an empty plate. Tien walked over and pointed toward the guy in the middle of the room. Obviously he was very popular with some ladies because they hovered around him like flies around molasses.

"You see that guy; he's not famous, yet! You'll know his name soon enough, as he just signed up for a major part in an upcoming big budget movie. Come on, I'll introduce you to the crowd."

As we walked closer I overheard him say to the women surrounding him,

"I think a woman is at her sexy best when she throws her head back and shakes her long hair, then, ever so lightly brushes it off her face..."

I couldn't keep myself from staring at this guy. For an Asian guy he was tall, rail thin with more hair than me. Back in those days he sounded cheap and condescending. He continued by asking, "When do you think a guy looks cool or the sexiest?"

Nobody says a word I stopped and asked him this question, "You mean when a man thinks he looks so incredible sexy to the women?"

He threw his hand up, "Yes, you've got it!"

All the women eyes were fixed on me. I imitated a movement and said, "Maybe when he pulls out a cigarette with one hand and flips open his Zippo with other to light it."

His eyes popped out of his head. I was some kind of hero to him at that moment and he said incredulously, "Ladies, she's the first one to get it right!"

I did my best to keep my face straight when I replied, "That was a no brainer, judging by the smoke in this room."

The funny part of this is that he thought I was sincere. What a freak!

The reason I brought my adopted sister into this book and this is very important for me to point it out; she was the first and only one ever to take me out onboard the famous floating restaurant on the Saigon River. This fancy eating place was legendary and only affordable to the higher class.

That was a beautiful evening and we sat outside in the open air with a warm with soft breeze. The water of the river was shining and shimmering beneath hundreds of light bulbs. She grins, watching my right hand tracing alongside the pristine white table cloth, then touching the velvet red roses in the center. I'm sure there must have been tears in my eyes at that moment as I whispered to her, "This place is beautiful! Almost like magic!"

We were talking and laughing nonstop. Not even once did she talk about the old days, clearly she left it all behind. Just like any other generation, we gossiped about celebrities. She had dirt on several and I listened with glee. I was having so much fun; I was high without even one drop of alcohol.

That was an awakening experience to me, about life, relationships, social status, and darn good food all at once. So when that night ended Tien told me to pick a path and try to stick to it.

The Vietnamese's language is not that simple. For example: the word, Tien, with a half square mark and an incline slanted over the e means money.

The very same word minus the slant translates into English as angel.

Shrimp Toast

This dish always reminds me of Sunday brunch in Saigon, a Vietnamese classic!

The aroma brings back happy memories of when I was younger and at a different place.

1lb of raw shrimp, peeled
1 small bulb of garlic, peeled
1 medium sweet onion or 4 shallots
1T cornstarch
1egg white
1T oyster sauce
1/2t each salt and pepper
1t sugar
2 Stalks of scallion
Hand full of cilantro, 1- 2 fresh hot chilies (option)

In a food processor, pulse on and off until all ingredients are coarsely chopped. At this point, the whole thing can rest in the refrigerator from 1hr to 24 hours. Have one cup of Panko breadcrumbs ready.

Cut across a loaf of French bread to 1/2 of inch thick slices. With a knife spread shrimp paste over each slice, smooth the top and dip that side into the breadcrumbs.

In a large skillet with medium heat, drizzle in enough oil to make a thick coat, cook the shrimp side first. When that's golden and the shrimp mixture is cooked through, turn over, and add more oil as needed to brown the other side. Serve it as it is or with the sauce below.

Hoisin and chili sauce

1/4 cup hoisin sauce
2T Sriracha or your favorite hot sauce
A touch of hot oil, garlic oil or sesame oil, you pick!

The Sandwich Diet

I lived in Long Beach California when I first arrived from Viet Nam. Being single with a job in this city, I had no complaints. I had a lot of fun with my gal friends who included quite a few Vietnamese, a couple of Korean girls and one Filipino in our circle and we were hanging out more than we should.

Weekends always consisted of eating out, shopping for clothing that we didn't need, going to Las Vegas to play Black Jack, and hitting the beaches.

After an exhausting trip over one weekend we were brainstorming trying to think of new things to do but sadly only food was on our collective mind, so the Eating Club was born. Each member took turns hosting on Sunday afternoon.

During this stage of my life I called myself Lisa, courtesy of a hit song, to better blend in with Americana.

My best friend in the club was another Vietnamese girl, Seanna. Of course it wasn't her real name. She put a dozen names she liked in a large mixing bowl, tossed it up and Seanna she became. We shared an apartment for a couple of months before I got my own place. We got along very well. We both liked to cook. Seanna wasn't the sharpest tool in the shed but she was sweet and I adored her. The second week of our rooming together she proposed an idea.

"We're getting fat from eating so much rice, how about we go on a sandwich diet? Let's just try it for a week; we might shed a few pounds, would you like to join me?"

All my chubby life I've had this fantasy of losing ten more pounds not matter what I weighed so I happily jumped in, no questions asked.

The first day I almost fainted when I saw the sandwich she laid on the table.

A big fat loaf of Italian bread filled to the top with all kinds of cold cuts, pickles, and peppers. She cut it in half, I looked at my half then I looked at her, totally in disbelief,

"Seanna, I will not eat all that!

She looked at the piglets in the form of an Italian sandwich on our plates and chuckled,

"Maybe it is a bit more food then we need but since this is our first day we should ease ourselves into the ordeal and prevent the body from shock." She continued,

"Tomorrow we will definitely cut way, way down!"

She was obviously full of it and the proof was the big loaf of crispy French bread all bulked up with fire grilled beef with all the trimmings. One glorious pound of flank steak marinated with lemon grass, garlic, chilies, all dolled up with scallion oil, and sweet and sour carrots.

She stared at the sandwich and declared, "Half of it is mine, you better cut it equally or someone is going to get hurt".

"I'll try to be fair, but, if you think you're going to get a bigger piece than you're wrong" I said laughing.

The delicious fragrance of the beef with cilantro, hot peppers and the rest only added to our joy of eating. We were so busy chewing and swallowing. This is hard work I thought as I watched beads of sweat roll from her brow.

"I like this diet!" She gushed.

"Me too, but I don't have to be an expert on diets to know we are not making any progress by eating this much!"

"OK, we'll downsize the sandwich tomorrow." She agreed.

Of course, we both lied through our teeth. The following day we made the most famous of all Vietnamese sandwiches, one with a lot of French influence. It's made with real butter, ham pate and all the traditional Vietnamese trimmings. We inhaled that 24 inch sandwich with much bliss nonetheless.

Monday morning arrived, we were getting ready to go the work and I watched her slide across her bed and try to zip up her jeans. She sounded totally irritated,

"Let's hope I over-dried these damn pants."

"Maybe we are just bloated with all the back up from not eating our vegetables?"

I said with false hope. I hadn't lost an ounce, anything but. It was totally the other way around. However I did have great time and I don't regret it.

Steamed Buns with Pork, Chicken and Shiitake Mushroom

My children grew up on this item. They never thought much of it, until they were on their own. Then they realized how special a homemade bun was compared to the stuff they bought in China Town or anywhere else. Like any good food it takes a bit of work and organization but when you bite into this soft and fluffy bun fresh out of a steamer, you'll know there is no substitute.

The science behind this dish is very simple; soft lightly sweet bread wrapped around a moist and delicious meatball, slightly on the salty side to form a harmony of taste.

A large steamer is required in this project.

Buns

1cup warm water
1 package of dry yeast
1T vegetable oil
3 cups flour
2t baking powder
1/2 cup sugar

1t salt
Extra flour for dusting

Make dough the way you do bread, start with warm water, stir in yeast, mix well, adding the rest and knead until smooth and elastic. This process should take about ten minutes. Set dough in a greased bowl and place it in a warm place, free of drafts. Let it rise for two hours.

Filling
2 hard boil eggs, cut into 8 pieces set aside
8 pieces of wax papers, 4x4, set aside
8oz ground pork
1 boneless chicken breast, coarsely chopped. (Approximately) 4oz
4 large dried Shiitake mushrooms, soaked until soft and coarsely chopped.
1/ 4 cup coarsely chopped baby Bella mushrooms
1/4 cup petit peas
1 egg white
2t cornstarch
1T rice wine or dry sherry
2T oyster sauce or light soy sauce
3/4t each salt and freshly ground black peppers
2 t toasted sesame oil

In a large mixing bowl, gently mix the ground pork with rest of the above ingredients. Let filling rest in the refrigerator until dough is ready.
Start by punching the dough down, gently roll it into a rope, cut this rope into 8 pieces, then form each piece into a ball. Lightly dust them with flour, cover with pastry cloth, and let it rest for 30 minutes. Lightly dust counter surface with flour and roll each ball into 6 inch circles; for a better bun appearance make it thinner at the edge.
Next divide filling equally into 8 parts. An ice cream scoop makes an ideal for tool for this job.
Place each scoop of filling in a circle of dough, gathering up the outside of the dough make small pleats in a sweeping motion going all around, then bring together with a final twist and seal it all at the top of the bun.
Place bun on top of a piece of reserved wax paper.
Fill 2/3 of the bottom steamer with water plus 2T spoons of white vinegar* and bring it to a rolling boil, situated buns into upper part of steamer and cook for 25 minutes.
Now, it's ready to serve. A dollop of hoisin sauce, a family favorite, and some hot pepper paste, only if you want to give it an extra kick. That's the way my family eats them.

*The vinegar in water is an option to give bun a pristine white look. That's all!

Meat Loaf for Pot Luck

She's a world traveler, one week in Korea the next in England, but when she's at home, I most likely see her at our market.

She showed up one day and said unenthusiastically,

"Guess what? I'll have to cook sometime".

"Since when do you have to cook?" I asked.

"Well, my husband and I were at our annual meat loaf pot luck last night. He really liked one of the meat loaves someone prepared at the party. He took a second look at where the recipe came from and told me I better start learning to cook because he knows I got your book and that's where the recipe was from."

"I guess you have no other choice", I chuckled!

The meatloaf recipe she was referring to is featured in my first book. As far as I know it's popular with the folks who tried with all their might to avoid tofu.

I had known her since I first started out at Farmer's Markets. Our relationship stemmed back to the beginning - the earliest parts of my days when I was just starting out. I know exactly what she likes as far as food goes and beyond that. Since she was doing a lot of traveling, eating out was in the package. She would share culinary information which she knows interests me and I was truly grateful for what we had until recently she got an offer toward a big career change that required her to move out of Maine.

Even though I've known for a while that time would come for us to say goodbye, it still didn't make it any easier. I was trying with the all my might not to cry, and then I spotted a sparkle of a tear behind her sunglasses and that is where I let my emotions free. For the rest of that day, the emptiness wouldn't leave me. A good friend is hard to come by and so is great customer, she was both.

Stuffed Grape Leaves with Beef

I'm not a big fan of the hamburger, but I will make an exception when our grapevines are loaded with beautiful green leaves. If you can't get access to fresh leaves, the ones packed in brine at a special food store will work as well. Just rinse them out before use.

For better result, use the outdoor grill.

2 dozen large grape leaves
1lb of lean ground beef
1T chunky peanut butter

1 small onion, chopped
1 small bulb of garlic, peeled, chopped
2 fresh hot Jalapeno peppers (or 2T bell)* minced
1T scallion oil or vegetables oil
1T oyster sauce
1T soy sauce
1t each black pepper and sugar

Wash the grape leaves and blanch in boiling water for 30 seconds, rinse. Set aside.

In a large mixing bowl combine ground beef with the rest of the ingredients. Lay leaves down, and divide beef mixture to the narrow end of each leaf. Fold in both sides and roll it up as you do egg roll (or burrito). Brush with oil and grill over medium heat for 6 to 8 minutes, turn once.

*Only for someone who can't handle the heat.

Beef in Orange Sauce with Cashew

Every now and then this dish will appear at my table.

I'm not a big fan of beef but I'll make room for this dish. It is smooth, spicy, and aromatic. The dried orange peel makes for a sweet and tangy sauce.

Meat

In the medium bowl, mix well and set aside

1-1 1/2lb of flank steak, slice thin
2T rice wine
1/2t each salt, black pepper, and sugar
2T tapioca flour
2T corn starch
2t sesame oil
This step can be done a day ahead
Spices for taste (and smell)
2T crushed garlic
2T dried hot peppers flake
1 large orange, gently grate the outer peel, reserve juice
3 stalks scallion cut ½ inch

Sauce

Mixed in small bowl with the orange juice

1/4 cup soy sauce
3T sugar

3T rice vinegar
2 cups oil for blanch beef
1/2 cup of cashew

In a wok with high heat, bring oil to 350 degree, and test with a piece of scallion. If the onion surfaces as soon as you drop it into oil, the oil is ready for action.

Divide beef into three parts, drop in hot oil, being careful, break and swirl it around, soon as beef almost lose the pink, remove it with a mesh spoon and place it over a stainless steel colander. Make sure a small bowl is placed underneath to catch the dripping oil.

When all beef has been blanched, remove most of oil; stir fry the cashew until lightly brown. Remove cashew to a small bowl. Set it aside.

Back to the hot wok with garlic, orange peel and hot pepper, stir fry until fragrance but not brown, add beef, take 1-2 minutes here - depending on the heat of your stove- pour in sauce and lets it all bubble up, stir well, drop in the crispy cashew and remove wok from heat. Add the scallion and serve at once.

*Added bonus point of this dish; you can do it as appetizers, simply fry the beef until crispy. Make the sauce and use it for dipping.

Bird of All Seasons

The Stud Muffin from Stonington

That was a warm, breezy, beautiful Fourth of July weekend in Deer Isle. This kind of day would easily draw all kinds of people to our Farmer's Market, and it did.

They stopped at my table and admired the food display. A young man with an extra small tank top; its sole purpose was to show off his wash board abs. Shoulder to shoulder with him is a portly middle aged man in a colorful shirt. The young man was nodding his head; his earring rocked with the motion of his bobbling gesture, his voice was excited as his gaze traveled along the table full of food.

"Wow! It's smells really good here. I want some"

"But Tiger we just had breakfast," the older man protested.

"Lunch will come soon; besides who says you can't eat one meal right after another."

The young man is grinning from ear to ear like a kid in the middle of a candy store. The (almost) senior citizen said nothing, but he reached into his pocket and pulled out a large bill, which he quickly shoved it into the stud muffin's hand then walked away. I don't know why sometimes I like to get involved into other people's business and this was one of those times. In my defense, in this particular case, the young man was more eager to open himself up whether it was to me or to anyone that happened to be there.

As I was dishing out Tiger's order (and he wants a lot) we started to chat. I have to give him all the credit of how easy it was for me to talk to him.

It was like a visit from a friend.

"Tell me if I'm wrong because I don't think I have ever seen you before" I said.

"No, you are right, we're just passing through," He smiled and flashed his even and white set of teeth. He's boyish and actually cute.

"Where are you going?"

"We are heading to Canada"

"What are you guys going to do in Canada?" I should not have asked that question.

"Anything that my heart desires," he was beaming. Something in the way he said it made me take the conversation to a totally different direction. With a mischievous grin I asked

"Do you always get what you want?"

"Hell yes!"

"Hey more power to you Tiger" I said as I handed him a large brown bag.

Since he purchased a large order, I rewarded him with a couple of egg rolls; he crunched right into it and gushes, "Man, this is really good. I'll stop by on my way back to visit you again."

"Hey, that would be nice! Then you can tell me everything you do in Canada"

"Not everything" He grins.

I called to him as he walked away, "Tiger, be kind to the loved one, okay?"

He pats his bag of goodies still grinning, "Always!"

I made a new friend because he kept his word to visit me after their trip, with a cooler between his arms, and a bigger order.

I asked "Are you going to eat all that?"

He rolls his eyes, "Unfortunately for me" he raised both arms making air quotations; "the loved one likes it more than I do."

The loved one was standing right behind the stud muffin. A broad smile was on the loved one's face as he nodded his head.

Something good must have happened in Canada.

The Wise Man

John and I share the Orono market. He owns and operates Mainely Poultry.

Whenever I can, at the market, I like to park next to John for more than one reason. More often than not he helps me set up my tent because I'm usually late to arrive. It only takes me thirty six minutes from my house versus his two hours, something is terribly wrong with this picture. The second reason I like to park next to John is if the market happens to be slow that day I'll automatically behave. It has got to do with his laid back appearance that stops my desire to whine and complain. I like John, and I want to preserve our friendship. So, by keeping my mouth shut I save our friendship. I protect my friends anyway I can, especially from myself. The third and most important reason I park next to John is that we never fail to make each other laugh. We can be disagreeing over current affairs, relationships, or human behavior but we always have a jolly time over these issues nonetheless. There is one thing we will always agree on: the time we spend at the market is actually down time because as soon as we get home, chores are waiting for us. This recipe requires quality chicken, the kind you can count on from John's farm.

Mainely Chicken
1 large chicken about 5 lbs
1t salt, 1t black pepper
1/4 cup fresh ginger julienne cut
2T dark brown sugar
1/3 cup Mirin or rice wine
1/4 cup light soy sauce and 1T dark soy sauce

Preheat oven to 350 degree.
Grease a 9 by 12 baking pan
Rinse chicken, pat dry, cut it at all joints, reserve backbone for soup stock. You'll have two wings, two thighs, 2 drum sticks, cut breast into quarters. You'll have four pieces of breasts. Mix chicken with salt and pepper then place them in a prepared baking pan.

In a medium sauce pan, caramelize brown sugar, important not to burn, as soon as the color changes add ginger then wine and soy sauce, bring it to boil and let it simmer for few minutes, pour sauce over chicken, swirl around, cover up with foil then put it in the oven for 45-50 minutes. Half way through, turn meat over and remove foil.

Sauce should perfectly cling to every piece of meat. Serve with plenty of rice and steamed vegetables.

Sometimes I squeeze half of lime and a few drops of hot sauce over the chicken before I serve. These simple touches change the taste of this dish on a whole new level.

My Diet Ordeal
The time was right after Thanksgiving when I couldn't get into my jeans, so I decided go on a diet. It was a somewhat traumatic experience for me.

At eight o'clock in the morning after that historic day, I prepared a healthy breakfast with 2 egg whites, mushrooms and spinach, cutting the process (and calories) down by using cooking spray- not my usual shallot oil. I was so proud of myself for forcing this lean omelet down and swallowing every last awful bite. Around 10am, just like any good diet allows, I ate a carrot and a stalk of celery, instead of the usual bar of dark chocolate with raspberry, which was hidden safely in the bottom of the vegetable bin. It did the trick, because by 12 I was not very hungry but like I said I was on diet. I made myself a sensible green salad with plenty of chunk tuna. I did however leave out the bacon, so I stayed on track. This salad took the place of my usual big bowl of rice with all the trimmings. The lunch disappeared quickly, and I was so impressed with my willpower. At 1:30 I heard the items I truly wanted calling for me. No, I thought to myself! I have to stick with what I set out to do. I tried to tidy up the kitchen here and there while thinking of rice as being cold and dull. But before I know it I looked up at the dinner table and there laid a big bowl of rice and it wasn't cold and hard the way I forced myself to think about it at 1:30. The glistening Jasmine rice wasn't alone; it nested seductively next to a steamy bowl of chicken with ginger and saffron. It was left over from last night and I must have just heated it up unconsciously. I might as well put it to use. My whole diet ordeal lasted 5 hours and 56 seconds. That was the only time I attempted serious dieting and I failed!

Chicken with Ginger and Saffron
To prep the meat

2lbs of chicken breast cut into 1inc cubes
1/2 t salt, 1/2 t black pepper
1T cornstarch
1T garlic oil or vegetable oil

In a medium bowl mixed well, set aside.

Vegetables and spices
1 sweet onion cut into cubes
2 bell peppers cut into cubes
A pinch of saffron
2T fresh grated ginger
2T brown sugar
2T brandy or rice wine
2T light soy sauce
1T dark soy sauce
1/2 cup chicken stocks

In wok with high heat, swirl in 2T oil, when a wisp of smoke appears; add chicken and move it quickly all around to brown it evenly, toss in ginger and saffron, take time between each ingredient.

When the aroma of ginger and saffron fully surface, sprinkle in sugar, let it caramelize before drizzling in the brandy, wait a little time here before tossing in onion, peppers, soy sauce and broth. Cover it up, cook from 3 to 4 minutes. Chicken should be cooked through, but vegetables should be firm and crisp, so it can be good and ready to reheat the next day if you plan to be on a diet.

Note: I really do believe this dish tastes even better the next day and so does my family.

The Famous Chicken

She slowed down and peered at my table then asked, "Do you have any General Tso's chicken?"

"No, I'm sorry, I don't do that dish," I said it politely.

"Why not," she pressed.

"Well, I choose not to because it's too fattening, I have a dish of chicken right here and it tastes much better without any extra breading and so much leaner."

"But I want the fat," she said curtly.

A male customer gives her some advice: "Listen, when you leave this parking lot, turn left, keep going and whenever you see any sign for a Chinese restaurant, you'll find the chicken you want"

She gave him an unfriendly stare then stomped off to her car, the man then said sincerely, "Thank you for not making that "famous" fattening chicken"

"Thank you for giving her the direction to find it" I exhaled.

Thank god he saved me from saying something to that woman which I know for certain I would have regretted.

The Not So Famous General Nga's Chicken

I actually feel very bad for General Tso's name. It has been dragged across all menus in Americanized Chinese restaurants in the States. Often, this dish poorly represents classic Chinese cuisine and what it really stands for.

In fact, in this country he has more than one name, let's see, there were General Tsao, Gau, Cho, Ching and the list goes on and on. So what's wrong with General Nga?

Was there ever a General Tso in Chinese history? There was in the nineteenth century but I doubt very much that his favorite dish of chicken would taste anything like the kind all of America finds in their neighborhood Chinese eateries. I'm neither a General nor am I famous but I know what I want out of a simple dish of chicken. Here is my version of this well-known dish and I hope whenever you're in the mood for something sweet and spicy with a bit of a kick, you can actually make it for yourself.

Start with 1lb of boneless chicken breast or boneless chicken thigh; remove all visible fat and membranes, cut into 3/4 of an inch cubes, then toss well in the marinade described below.

Meat

1 egg
1/4 cup corn starch
1/2t each salt and pepper
2t sesame oil

This step you can do a day ahead, cover and give it a rest, at least 20 minutes.

Oil for deep fry, you may use peanuts oil here if you wish. About 4 cups
Extra corn starch for dust

For the spices
2t minced garlic
1T fresh grated ginger
1/4 cup scallion for garnish

Sauce
2T brown sugar
2T hoisin sauce
1T hot pepper sauce*
2T good rice wine or sherry
1T rice vinegar
1T each dark and light soy sauce
1/4 cup chicken stock

In a wok with high heat, pour in oil and heat it up to 350 degree, remove chicken from its marinade, drag each piece into corn starch and fry- in batches- until almost cook through, avoid overcooking meat, remove into a bowl, set aside.

Drain oil-leave about 1 Table spoon remain in wok-to a heat proof container and save it in refrigerator for later use.

Back to the hot wok with ginger and garlic, spend a little bit of time here until you can detect the aroma, next in line is the brown sugar. Swirl it around until it's lightly caramel then adding hoisin sauce follow by chicken pieces, drizzle in the wine, and slowly pour in hot sauce and the rest of ingredients. Bring it all to boil about 2 to 3 minutes. Sauce should cling nicely to meat and not be runny. Toss in scallion and serve with rice and steamed vegetables.*I use Sriracha hot chili sauce in this dish..

The Devoted Customer
Out of nowhere, he appeared at my table four weeks in a row. I noticed him mostly because he purchased one item at a time, eating his way through the whole table. He must have thought that this mode of action was original. Sorry Mister, but others have done that before you. As he consumed his goodies, he was also busy making sales pitches to the people already in line. I noticed some of my regular customers becoming annoyed by it but for the most part they just ignored him. Through on and off conversations he told me he was a musician. His band traveled throughout the East coast to perform at

corporate private parties, fancy restaurants, etc. I listened to his story with a grain of salt.

Then, at the end of fourth week he made his move, "Hey! I know you are busy and all but how about taking a break to see my band play in Boston next week." He leaned against the corner of my tent and winked seductively.

"Well, that's sounds wonderful! I'll let my husband know, so he can clear his calendar for your special invitation," I said it with a grin. He was busy with a piece of chicken in his mouth but at that moment he stopped chewing altogether. A peculiar look flashed across his face as he walked away. If you guessed that I never saw this guy again then you are correct!

(Oven) Fried Chicken

The first take out meal I ever ate came from Kentucky Fried Chicken. My friend LAN* and I were dining inside her brother-in-law's car that was in the parking lot outside the Los Angeles' hospital. She was sad because her husband was dying. I wasn't happy either, however I was glad because at that moment I thought to myself, "at least I know one person, and I have a meal."

I think you'll find my chicken better with its coating of corn starch and egg whites crafted to give a very crispy and tasty crunch and you miss the frying and cleaning process.

1 frying chicken, 4 to 5 lb rinsed, dried off and cut up.

Paste
2 cloves of garlic
2 shallots
2t salt
1t black pepper
1T sugar
2T onion oil or vegetables oil
1t hot oil (option)

In a food processor, puree all the ingredients above into a smooth paste. Rub paste to coat chicken parts. Chicken may be marinated from 2 hours to overnight.

Coating
2 eggs white
2T cornstarch
1cup Panko breadcrumbs

Beat eggs white until foamy, fold in cornstarch. With pastry brush, put a light coat of this mixture into each piece of chicken; next roll them into Panko breadcrumb and bake in the oven of 350 degree for an hour or until juice runs clear.

Variation of fried chicken

For Thai hot: add a hand full of cilantro and 2 to 3 fresh chili to the paste.

*I talked about LAN in my first book, whom I met on the flight from Viet Nam.

That's enough!

She'll always be remembered by my daughter Sam and me as the "that's enough" lady. She seemed so small and frail and her walk was so slow. Sam and I were both fearful she might just fall over when the Bar Harbor wind started acting up. To make matters even more nerve racking she would carry a cane, but only on certain days. She was such a faithful customer she would sometimes visit us twice a week, Thursdays at North East Harbor then again on Sundays at Eden. Sam usually spotted her from a distance, and then would whisper to me, "Here comes "that's enough lady". Here's the deal: the entrée dishes could be purchased in eight, sixteen, or thirty-two ounce sizes. However we had to make an exception for her. It seemed like as soon as we started to dish out food into the container her arms would shoot out across her body like a lightning rod. They would slash into the air with such force that it surprised us every single time and she would say it in her special raspy voice, "That's enough!"

Sam can do a perfect imitation of her voice. She can easily mimic the ways the "that's enough lady" would take forever to form her decision and then only seemed to want a bite-sized portion. Sometimes, when I happen to be in a bad mood all Sam has to do is perform this act and I can't help but to burst into laughter. So, Sam and I had this little game going between the two of us. Since Sam is young and very impatient and I am old but constantly moving, the game was to see who could get away from serving this special customer. Well, Sam was always fast and cleverly moved to the next one in line almost every time and then she would giggle afterward because she had won the game. Most of the time she won the game fair and square but there were times I just let her win. Then one summer we didn't see this special customer and by August Sam said to me,

"Mom, the "that's enough lady" hasn't shown up yet this year".

"I know," I said to her, "she's probably late this year, we just have to wait and see". She didn't show up the following year as well. I miss her and I believe Sam does too. She once told me that if the "that's enough lady" shows up that she wants to be the one to wait on her! I told her that would be fine but she'd have to beat me to it.

The game was on but "that's enough lady" never showed.

Sweet and Spicy Chicken

Watch the sugar glow in this dish. The "that's enough lady" loves it, but she'd never wanted anymore than three or four pieces.

Chicken

1 and 1/2 to 2lbs of boneless chicken thigh cut into cubes and mixed well with the spices below

1t cinnamon
1/4t clove
1/2t each salt and peppers
2T cornstarch
2T garlic oil or vegetables oil
1T chili garlic paste (option)

This step can be done a day ahead

Spices and vegetables
2T-crushed ginger
1 green bell pepper cut into small cubes
1 red bell pepper cut into small cubes

Sauce
1/4 cup raw sugar or dark brown sugar
1/4 cup rice wine or sherry
1/4 cup soy sauce
1/2 cup broth

The garnish
1/4 cup lightly toasted pine nut
Juice of 1 lemon
Cilantro or herb of your choice

If chicken has been in refrigerator overnight, bring it to room temperature before show time. In a wok with high heat (or large nonstick skillet) swirl in a thin layer of oil, when oil start to smoke, brown chicken pieces. Make it two or three batches if you have too. When the last batch is done, return all chicken back to wok sprinkle sugar around wok and let it caramelize at the edge, at this point add ginger (not until you see some of the sugar brown and shine) allow the ginger to do its magic for about 1 to 2 minutes. Stir well, and then slowly add the wine. You cannot rush this step; this is the time frame needed to allow the dish to make its own identity.

Pour in broth and soy sauce, bring it to boil, cover and cook for 5 minutes. When time is up, add peppers, stir, and let sauce thicken. Toss in pine nut, herb and lemon juice. Serve at once. Rice would be an excellent choice!

Emma

We were brought together by destiny; an Easter egg hunts twenty something years ago. My children were young then and she just happened to be there volunteering. We clicked easily and it was effortless to be friends with one another. I have never been a good candidate to enter into any relationship, mostly because when I work I tend to neglect everything else. Emma knows all my flaws and loves me anyway. She's sweet and generous. Most of her free time is spent volunteering. I wish I could be like her, but it's not me.

I dedicate this dish to my friend because it reflects on how I see her-classy!

Emma's Roasted Chicken with Lemongrass

I'll welcome a roasted chicken dinner any day. This one is a bit fancy but can stand in for a special occasion or a long weekend (especially when you'll need leftover for sandwiches).

Maine winters are always long so we require as much comfort as we can get. A piece of this spicy, exotic meat will fit for the bill.

1 good size roasting chicken, 6 to 7 pounds

Paste

3 stalks lemongrass, discard the tough part, slice thin
1 to 3 red Jalapeno peppers
6 cloves garlic, peeled
1 and 1/2t black pepper a bit less if you don't want it too spicy
2t each sugar and salt
2T garlic oil or vegetables oil

In food processor, turn these ingredients into a paste. Loosen up the skin as much as possible. Rub this paste all over the outer skin and inside the cavity as well as under the skin where possible.

At this point, it can be rest in refrigerator up to 24hrs. But, if time is an issue, 1 or 2 hours will do. Turn the oven to 425 degrees and roast it for 20 minutes then lower the heat to 350 degrees and cook for another hour and twenty minutes more. Chicken is cooked when the thickest part reads 185 degrees.

Jenny

She was a vendor of the Buck street market long before I entered the picture. She always welcomed me and my food with open arms. We became friends quickly. We saw life through the same eyes except when it came to preparing food. She was a gourmet cook in her own right and more often than not Jenny wanted me to taste everything she made. Of course she was cooking the white people food and quite often I enthusiastically cheered on her craft but then added my last opinion:

"It tastes great! But it's so fattening, do you have to make it with a stick of butter? Please, do yourself a favor and cut down on the fat."

She would flash her charming grin and say, "That's why I buy your food every Saturday."

"You still have to think about the rest of the week Jenny. Do the freaking math!" Nobody was more excited when my first cook book came out than Jenny. The week before we had our party to celebrate I got a call from her. Breathlessly she said, "Hey Bich Nga, guess what? I got a new car, I'll come to your party in style, a PT Cruiser, what do you think of that?" I congratulated her and told her I was looking forward to seeing her the following week.

At that point Jenny had already left the Buck Street market, so we hadn't seen each other at all. She told me she couldn't wait "I even went shopping for a new outfit for your party" she added. In the middle of greeting people and signing books, there was a call from Jenny. She said she was about to leave her house and asked for the directions. All day had passed and she had not arrived. The called came the week later and it was from her daughter. They had to rush Jenny to Boston for medical treatment-Colon cancer.

Jenny had collapsed just minutes before they left to head on toward my house.

"Please let me know when she's going to be home; so I can pay a visit," I told her daughter. I never got that chance. She passed away shortly after that and I lost a friend forever. I try not to cook anything with a stick of butter only to preserve her memory and the memory of our friendship. She loves this particular dish of roasted chicken. Here's to you, Jenny!

Roasted Chicken with Five Fragrances

This is another roasted chicken dish; I often cook for my every day eating, nothing fancy. But we all love it. The best part, when this bird in the oven, the whole house will smell with the wonderful aroma. Unless you don't like spices, that's a different story.

1 large roasting bird 6-7 pounds. Clean it out, rinse, dry thoroughly with paper towel

Oil mixture
2T garlic oil
2t sesame oil

2T rice wine or sherry
1t hot oil (optional)

Dry rub
 2t five spices powder
1T granulated garlic
1T brown sugar
2t coarse sea salt
1t hot pepper flakes-optional-
1t black pepper

Turn oven to 350 degrees.
 Use the same technique with the previous recipe; rub in oil first then dry spices.
Cook for 1 1/2 - 2 hours, depending on the performance of your oven. It may take a bit longer, or shorter, you'll know. Use your meat's thermometer, the temperature should reach185 degrees.

Angel on Fire
 We've known her since she was a toddler with long blond hair and fair skin. That's why we called her our little angel. All the vendors at that small market knew her mother as well and they visited us every Saturday like clockwork. Needless to say we adored our regular little guest and we had permission from her mother to give her samples at any time. One hot summer afternoon, when angel was about four years old, she blasted into market and made a frozen stop at my table. I noticed her face was as red as a fireball and she had the attitude to match. It seemed like she needed someone to vent on, to get out whatever was bothering her.
 So I volunteered, "What's the matter sweetie? You don't look very happy!"
 "I don't know what the hell my mother is cooking for dinner because the whole house smells like chicken sh-t," she blurted out along with the huffs and puffs while both of her hands were wrapped around her body.
 Believe me, I wasn't the only one shocked by this outburst. Both vendors and customers all turned their heads to my spot.
 I didn't know how to respond to this but I knew I wanted to lighten her mood so I said, "Oh come on, there's lot of foods that don't smell so hot but taste delicious.
 Like cheese for example, some varieties actually make an old sock smell like roses". She didn't crack a smile. By then, her mother came in with her basket. Our little angel turned to her mother and pointed at the chicken with wine and ginger dish, "Old mom, this is what I want for dinner, please!"

Trust me, the lady was not anywhere near old and she wasn't present for any part of angel's outburst. But the mother smiled sweetly at her daughter and said, "Are you still mad?"

Angel felt better (I could tell) after her mother handed her the container of her request. Of course, the vendors' roared with conversation after they left. I had to jump in to defend our little angel "Give her a break!" I said, "You would be angry too if you had to eat chicken poop for dinner."

Special Duck

Any dinner with duck is special. Around here if you are craving a good piece of duck then you'll have to roll up your sleeves and go to work, just like I do.

1 good size duck 5 to 6 pounds, rinse, dry with paper towel. Place duck with breast side up on top of a rack. Place rack over a roasting pan then place pan inside refrigerator for at least 24hrs. Every now and then turn duck over and don't cover it. As matter of fact you have to make sure the air is circulated around the bird. This process will create a crispier skin. Have these herbs ready before show time

Herbs and spices for inside duck

A large chunk of ginger, crushed
A hand full of cilantro
3 stalks of scallion cut in half
Zest of small orange, strips with no white part

Paste
1/4 cup chicken broth
2T rice wine or sherry
1T soy sauce
1T oyster sauce
1T tomatoes paste
2T honey
2T corn syrup
2t five spices powder
2t sesame oil
Black pepper to taste

In food processor puree the above ingredients into a smooth paste.
Preheat oven to 425 degree.
Stuff the herbs inside duck cavity; place it directly with breast side up over the rack of a roasting pan. Roast duck in this high temperature for about 20 minutes, turn it over and continue for 15 minutes more. At this point, lower

temperature to 325 degree and roast it 45 minutes longer. Baste with paste every 10 minutes at the last 40 minutes.

Remove it from the oven the finishing bird should be shinning -courtesy of the corn syrup in the paste- with crispy skin.

Let it rest for 10 minutes before you carve and enjoy!

Use the remaining paste for dipping, or use hoisin sauce instead. There are many ways to serve this bird, thin scallion pancake, rice noodles with scallion oil, or my favorite way plain rice and steamed vegetables.

Scallions Pan Cakes
1 and 3/4 cups bread flour
3/4 cup boiling water
1/2t salt
1T chopped scallion
2t sesame oil

In a medium bowl and a wooden spoon mix flour, salt and scallion with hot water. Move spoon with one direction until flour absorbs all liquid. Knead dough into a ball, cover, and rest for 30 minutes.

In a floured surface, shape dough into a rope and divide into 12 pieces.

Roll each piece into 6 to 7 Inches in diameter, lightly brush with sesame oil and cook in a skillet with medium heat until bubble and lightly brown at both side. As any quick bread, serve it soon as you can.

Market Fun Day
It was a warm and sunny early summer's day at the Orono market and the line at the front of my table was long.

It's doesn't matter which market it is during July and August, there's always a line. I often apologize to my patience customers who wait a long time to be served. But they all seem to say the same thing, "That's ok. You're worth it".

This kind of comment makes my job so rewarding.

This day the line was mostly young females so he stood out like a sore thumb. I noticed him right away in the midst of the young ladies.

Tall and cute he had a leash dangling at his hand attached to a well trimmed Yorkshire Terrier with a hot pink bow on top her head. Of course, one can only stand so much ooh and ahs over a dog (or her owner).

When it came his turn he didn't waste any second on talk, "I had some of your fresh rolls last week. It was so good that I had to come back for more before I leave to go home."

"Well, thank you! I'm glad you enjoyed them. Where do you come from?"

"New York," he smiles, flashing his pearly whites.

"Really, what do you do in the big city?"

"I'm a chef," he said.

I decided to entertain my young female audience. With winking eyes I said, "Ladies, he's young, cute and he's a chef. What do you guys think of that? And I don't see any ring on his finger".

I heard some chuckling from the crowd and I could tell they were having fun, him included. When the young blonde lady right behind him raised her hand and said

"I'm available". He had a grin so wide it almost made his face split in half.

"So, what's your specialty?" I usually ask that question to someone when they say they're in the food industry.

"Italian cuisine I make a mean Fricasseed chicken," he replied, beaming.

"Really, with dried Porcini mushroom and Marsala wine or the Abruzzi style with white wine, cherry tomatoes, olive and Rosemary. There are so many ways to play with that dish, which one are you talking about?"

He shook his head impressed, "Wow! You know Italian cuisine".

"A little bit", I shrugged.

We chatted some more about food (which I really do enjoy) and he picked up his package waved good bye to the ladies and walked away into the bright sun. I turned to my audience "Sorry, girls, he's taken! What kind of single or normal guy would walk around with a dog that is that high maintenance?"

Chicken with Rosemary, Cherry Tomatoes and Black Olives

This is an absolutely stunning dish, the contrast of brown chicken, colorful tomatoes and black olives. Don't like rosemary? No problem! Pick your own herbs. It's all good!

4 to 5lbs chicken cut into 8 pieces, dry well and set aside in a large bowl.

Paste

In food processor

1 large bulb of garlic, cleaned, about 5 to 6 cloves
1T fresh rosemary leaves
1t each: salt, black pepper and red crushed hot pepper (to suit your taste bud)
2T olive oil

With a pulse on and off puree spices until smooth and mix it with chicken pieces, let rest from an hour to overnight.

Sauce and vegetables
1/2 cup of broth or white wine (it's your call to make!)
1 pint of cherry tomatoes prefer mixed color
12 to 15 salty black olives

Always use high heat where the task calls for brown meat.

In a large non-stick skillet with heavy bottom and a thin layer of olive oil, brown the chicken pieces. Do not crowd pan, you want that burning edge, repeat it in two batches if you don't have a large skillet.

When this task has done, pour in wine (or broth) loosen every bit of the brown stuffs and make sure the bird is lovingly bathed in all that goodness. Cover, lower heat and simmer for about 30 minutes. Open it up; add the tomatoes and olive scatter them around chicken pieces and cook another ten minutes. Chicken should be cling nicely to sauce, adjust the sauce to your desire because you are the boss!

The Alcohol Factor

Why alcohol when you can just use broth or water?

Each type of alcohol contributed its own complex balance of acidity/or sweetness. Last, but not least the indispensable aroma. This is the reason why sometimes when people come to me for a catering job, the prices are different. You'll get what you are paying for. Where its qualities are heightened, the best of alcohol I can find is used.

The Hopeful One

The fourth Saturday in April means the winter market is over. Hooray! This is when we say goodbye to downtown and move back to our regular spot at the steam plant parking lot.

The sun was blazing and warm when he stopped at my table. He was standing there for a good five minutes. He looked over every dish, asked questions and finally made his choice.

"It's all looks good but I only come here for fresh peas and potatoes," he said.

My initial reaction was he's joking but the serious look in his face sent me into shock wave. Holy cow! I just couldn't believe he really meant it.

I tried hard to not to say anything at all. I can call myself all sorts of names but genius is not one of them and that goes for this guy too. I wondered if this guy even knew where in the world he was, California?!

"Are you from around here, sir?"

"All my life"

"Then you must know the ground is still frozen. Why don't you come back here in two months and try again. Maybe by then we'll have fresh peas and new potatoes for you." At that time there was still a blanket of snow covering my garden and because of Maine's unpredictable weather I hoped I wouldn't choke on my words over that particular statement. The hopeful man shook his head as he walked away. The sun was getting really hot as he strolled out of the parking lot. To be honest, I was fearful he might turn around and start looking for corn.

From the Sea

Yvonne and her Fine Catch

Yvonne was the best looking girl in our eating club. For an oriental girl she was tall and slender. She was lucky it was a freebie look, a part of her genes. She was always stylishly dressed. Nobody I knew would wear high heels to Kmart plus all the accessories. Well that's Yvonne!

She hooked up with her boss in Saigon. At that time, any civilian American who worked in Vietnam was a good catch. They had a long going affair before he finally divorced his American wife who was back in the states and married Yvonne.

The day she left Vietnam with her handsome and wealthy husband she was the envy of all her friends. They settled in California and lived in a gorgeous house by the beach.

It was a picture perfect day when she came home early from a good old business trip. She wanted to surprise her husband so she didn't call.

She walked into her stylish bedroom and there he was, with another woman, on top of her silky sateen black sheets. This woman is no stranger to Yvonne. She was his new secretary.

That old dog was performing the same old trick!

Yvonne was no dummy and she cleaned him out for all she could.

A beach house was one of her consolation prizes, that and the freedom to embrace single life again. When we were hanging out, she loved to cook. Many delicious meals were served outside on the breezy balcony of that beach house.

Steamed Crab Cake

This classic dish is from Northern Vietnam. It is something my mother used to make only when we had company because let's face it- from a perspective of a third world country, it's not cheap.

One time Yvonne made it with spider crab. It was so good that the memory stays with me even now.

Since I left California I haven't seen it around here. The fresh crab from Maine is not a bad item to substitute for spider crab. Still it's not quite as good!

1lb of fresh crabmeat
8oz of ground pork
5 -6 dried shiitake mushroom. Soaked for 1/2 an hour, chopped
One oz of bean thread (cellophane noodles) soaked, chopped
1/2 cup sweet onion, chopped
1/2 t each salt and pepper
3 eggs
1T scallion oil
1T fish sauce
1T oyster sauce
1/2 t sugar

In a large mixing bowl combine the above ingredients, mix well.

Sometimes I put it into loaf pan, cover up with foil, place pan on top of hot water bath and bake it in 350 degree oven, for an hour and fifteen minutes. Check it at 55 minutes point, if juice runs clear it's done.

To steam, pour mixture into a round heat proof dish and put it on top of the rack, place rack over wok, pour water until the mark reach over bottom of dish (1inc over).

Steam, over high heat for 45- 50 minutes. Pierce with chopstick in the middle, if juice runs clear dinner is ready.

My favorite way to serve this dish is sliced, and placed it over hot Jasmine rice. Drizzle with 2t scallion oil, shredded sweet and sour carrot and top it all with fish sauce dressing

The Old Fashion Way

They always arrived at my table hand in hand. If it was a windy day they'd lean on each other for support considering both of them were rail thin. It would be safe for me to say that they are my oldest pair of customers or as I like to express it, my two oldest diamonds.

Just before noon, week after week, month after month, I had the pleasure and honor to serve them their favorite dishes. They were not the kind of customers that jumped around the menu every time something new appeared. By their admissions, the husband always said, "I know we're boring but we want the same thing."

"Truthfully," I said, "it would be great if everybody was boring, it would be so much easier for me to plan the menu."

That's how I responded, and sincerely meant it. I always looked at them with admiration that truly came from my heart. These two people have been with each other their entire lives and what was beautiful about the whole thing was anyone could clearly see they were still crazy about each other. He looked at her with the adoration in his eyes and always referred to her as my dear wife.

She always tenderly nested against one side of his body, seldom spoke but when she did she would praised my work, and always make me feel that I was truly special to both of them.

Bear with me right here, because I'm about to side track you with a different story.

At the markets, although it's not often, I have seen a couple or two bickering in front of me and it usually makes me wonder: how much worse can they treat each other in the privacy of their own home. I've witnessed a husband and wife bark and sneer instead of talk and look at each other with disgust. For the most part if I see this happening I keep my mouth shut, except this one time. I knew I'd tick the husband off however, I just couldn't help myself.

A middle aged couple strolled by and the woman stopped at my egg roll sign and asked the man if she can have one, he refused her request with such an authority that it bothered me to no end. Before I knew it I was picking up a napkin and with a swift motion I grasped an egg roll and handed it to her, and I said it with a smug look, "Hey, if the lady would like to have an egg roll, she should! Here, it's on me."

There was more I wanted to say to this guy but I had to restrain myself. I'm so glad I did, otherwise I would have to put it all down and dirty my book in the process.

I could hear his neck snap as he turned around and stared me down. He was a big, angry man and I was ready for whatever he was going to throw at me, or her. No surprise but he only gave me a look that implied that I was not worth it for him to say anything, and then walked away followed by a frightful woman with an egg roll in her hand.

Anyway, back to the story of my two loving diamonds. She seldom spoke so he would be the one making small talk about weather or whatever was going on at the market. The most she ever said was, "We really like your food!" or "We get this much salad and it lasts all week long". No wonder they are so thin, maybe I should take note in this issue.

This is one line she said every week and it'll always be the line I cherish, "You are the only reason we come to the market" Nobody else says that to me, ever!

Then one day she let me get a glimpse into the secret of how their relationship worked. It was a stormy day, pouring rain; the wind blew through my skin like a razor. I looked up, and like clockwork they clung on to each other for support under a big umbrella. I shook my head at the husband and criticized jokingly, "I didn't expect you two to be here today. The weather is crazy! You shouldn't let her out of the house."

To his defense, she explained in a highly authoritative gesture, this was the most I had ever hear from this tiny little lady, "Well, he was the one that would rather be snuggled in his pajamas all day. I told him you are going to be at the market and I said, 'It's a rainy day! At least we can go to support her'". Then she smiled sweetly to me, "By the way, we're here just for you, dear".

I love the way she thinks and I can't help but adore this feisty woman. It's crystal clear, he might be wearing pants but she's the boss! And the boss lady adored her sea food.

Fish Stew with Tomatoes and Herbs

I like the taste of bouillabaisse but sometimes I just don't want to deal with wine and all of the fuss attached. So here is the alternative. This process makes me feel like I can have my cake and eat it too. On top of that, I also save some money. It's a win, win situation!

Fish
2lb of fresh white fish of your choice cut into cubes
1t each salt and pepper
2T garlic oil or vegetable oil

For the vegetables
2T olive or vegetable oil
1/2 cup chopped onion
1 cup chopped celery
1 large can crushed tomatoes (28 oz)

For the broth
2 cups broth
8oz clam juice
Cilantro or thyme for herb

Pat fish dry and mixed well with salt, pepper and garlic oil, set aside.

In a heavy bottom Dutch pan with 2T oil, sauté onion until lightly brown at the edge, add celery and cook until lightly soft. About five minutes. From there, tomatoes, clam juice and broth may be added and bring it all to boil. Gently put in fish, lower the heat and simmer for about 6-7 minutes.

Remove from heat before scattering in the herb.

I definitely serve a piping hot bowl of this fish stew with a crispy slice of French bread.

The Advice

He was always on time and purchased almost the same items week after week. Yes, he's one of my solid customers. When my first book hit the table he happily purchased it. Excitingly he said, "My wife's birthday is next week, this is perfect".

I just assumed the little lady loved to cook and the following week he showed up with a question, "My wife got your book. Now, what can I do so she can start to cook? I love fish, but she can't stand the smell, you have any advice for me?"

I had to use my brain for a second, "Give the lady a sincere compliment whenever she cooks. Kiss her every morning and tell her how pretty she is…"

He cut me right off

"I can't do that! Have you seen my wife?"

Actually I don't think I ever had. Now I'm curious.

Lazy Day Fish

Sometimes when I don't feel very motivated but I'm stuck with fresh fish that needs to be cooked, I turn to this dish. It's quick and it taste even better as left over.

2lbs white fish such as haddock cut into chunks
2 large bulbs of shallot sliced thin. Approximately 1/2cup
2T packed brown sugar
1/4 cup hot water
1/4 cup fish sauce
Generous amount of freshly ground black pepper
Fresh slices of hot peppers (option)

In the large, heavy Dutch pan (or skillet) with a thin layer of oil brown the shallots, remove set it aside. Put in the brown sugar, let the brown sugar bubble and caramelize, pour in hot water then fish sauce, stir until sauce thickens, about 1- 2 minutes. Return the brown shallot, toss in fish, spread it out in single layer, and mixed well. Cover pan, cook from five to seven minutes. Sprinkle with black pepper and serve it with rice and steamed vegetables.

Braised Fish with Eggplant, Tomatoes and Herbs

This dish is simple to prepare. I usually do it in the summer when the fresh tomatoes hang down from the vine, sweet and still warm from the sun. I turn around grab some fresh herbs, yank off a few young eggplants and dinner will be ready in just a few minutes. In the winter, it can be done with frozen tomatoes, herbs and substitute with different vegetables. Chayote squash from the super market is a good candidate to stand in for the job.

4 large fillets of white fish of your choice, around 1 1/2 - 2 lbs, rub with paste.

Paste
1 large bulb of garlic
1T shallot oil
1t each salt, pepper and sugar.

Toss fish gently with paste, let it rest, while prep the vegetables.

For the vegetables
3 large ripe tomatoes, chopped.
8oz clam juice
1lb of egg plant cut into cubes
1/2 cup of Thai basil or herb of your choice
Slices of hot peppers, option.

In a heavy bottom Dutch pan, or large skillet, bring tomatoes and clam juice to boil, arrange fish alternate with egg plant into sauce. Cover up; cook about seven to ten minutes. Taste, adjust the seasoning to your desired taste. Maybe a little bit more salt, depended on the tartness of tomatoes, a bit more sugar to make peace all around.

Don't overcook the egg plant. Remove from heat, before adding basil and hot peppers. Taste really good with rice.

Braising for the New Cook
Braising is the technique of slow cooking in liquid. Stocks or wine are needed for this type of cooking, and you will always need to cover it up with lid to retain moisture.

A heavy Dutch pan is perfect for this type of cooking.

Roasted Salmon with Wilted Greens
The wine and ginger will wash most of the unpleasant odor from fish, if there was one.

Marinate 2lbs of salmon fillet
Mix it in a stainless steel bowl
1/4 cup light soy sauce
2T rice wine, option!
2T garlic oil
1T crushed fresh ginger
2T brown sugar
2t sesame oil
Touch of salt and pepper

Wilting Greens
1lb of fresh spinach, washed and dried
1T vegetables oil
1T light soy sauce
Salt pepper to taste

Gently spread marinade over fish, keep it in the refrigerator from 1hour to overnight. Remove from liquid, discard the remaining juice.

Place fish in greased lined baking pan, and roast in preheated oven 400 degree, for about 20 minutes, fish should be easily to flake with a fork.

In a large skillet with oil and high heat, sauté spinach about 1-2 minutes, drizzle in soy sauce, season it with salt and peppers to your taste, and then turn heat off. Remove fish from oven, carefully lift it up, and place over a serving dish, cover fish up with spinach and serve. I suggest brown rice this time.

Creamy Scallops with Yellow Curry
This is one of my regular dishes belonging to the category of 10 minutes or less. You can serve it with hearty bread, rice, or noodles. Don't ask me, I'll pick rice any day.

Scallops
2lb of large scallop
1t salt
1/2t cayenne pepper
1T cornstarch
2t yellow curry

In a medium bowl mix the ingredients above well, set aside.

Vegetables
1 medium onion, cubed
1lb button mushroom quarters (or any fast cooking vegetables such as summer squash, sugar peas or baby Bok Choy)

Sauce
1 bottle of clam juice 8oz
1 can of coconut cream
Cilantro and sliced hot pepper for garnish, option.

In a Dutch pan or deep skillet with 2T of oil sear the scallop, drizzle a bit more oil as needed, put in onion take a little time here, vegetable go in next, then clam juice. Cover, cook for 2, to 3 minutes then add coconut cream.

When it boil again remove from heat, adjust the taste. Sprinkle with cilantro and hot peppers. Its goes well with rice.

Serve (4) or (6) depended on your generosity, there are plenty rice to go around and scallop is expensive!

Fish Steak in Tomatoes and Dill Sauce

Here is a comfort dish that is simple but elegant. I cook this dish often when the tomatoes ripen in the garden and I have the choices of all the colors I want. Dill can be used in this dish; cilantro also makes for another good candidate.

Don't stop there, use any herb you're comfortable with and make it your own signature dish.

Fish

4 (4 to 5 oz) each haddock, tuna, halibut or your favorite white fish
1/2t each salt and pepper
1/2t cayenne pepper (option)
1t each garlic, onion and hot oil

Coat fish steaks with the above ingredients, set aside.

For the aromatic and vegetables

4 thinly sliced shallots
4 large tomatoes cubes

Sauce

1 bottle of clam juice 8oz
2T fish sauce
A touch sugar (depended on tomatoes)

Garnish

A small bunch of scallion cut into 1inch long
Dill, cilantro or herb of your choice

In a large nonstick skillet with high heat and a thin layer of oil, lightly brown fish on both sides. Depending on the heat of your stove, this process can take from 6 to 8 minutes. Remove fish, back to skillet with shallot, drizzle a bit more oil if needed, sauté the shallot until it is lightly browned at the edge, add tomatoes, clam juice, fish sauce and bring it to boil for several minutes, until sauce a bit thicken. Return fish to skillet; let it simmer for about 5 minutes. Remove from heat before adding herb and scallion.

Beautiful Flounder
Quick, easy and delicious!

Fish
Heat oven to 350 degree
2lb fillet of fresh flounder
1/2t each salt and pepper
2T cornstarch
1 egg white
1/4 cup chopped scallion
1T scallion oil- or vegetable oil-

In a large bowl, beat up the egg white with cornstarch; fold in salt and pepper, oil and scallion. Mix well with fish and set aside.

Vegetables
1 large red bell pepper, sliced
1 large green pepper, sliced
8oz mushroom, sliced

Sauce
1/4 cup sweet cooking wine (Mirin)
2T light soy sauce
1T dark soy sauce
1T oyster sauce
2t sesame oil
2t dried hot pepper flakes (Option)

In 8x12 ovenproof dishes, arrange half of vegetables down, start with small end of flounder roll fish up and lay it on top of vegetable. Scatter the rest of mushroom and pepper on top, pour sauce evenly over all. Bake for 45 minute.

Skinny Shrimp
This dish may have Louisiana's footprint all over it, but you won't get the usual fat.

1lb of large shrimp, peeled, deveined

Spice mix for shrimp
1t each black pepper, cayenne pepper, sugar
Salt to taste or 1t
1/2t each; thyme and oregano

In a medium bowl mix shrimp with ½ of the spices plus 1T garlic oil and 1t hot oil.

Set aside.

Vegetables
1/2 cup chopped sweet onion
1/2 cup diced bell pepper
1cup chopped celery
1cup chopped tomatoes or sweet grape tomatoes cut in half

Sauce
2T vegetables oil
2T flour
1T hot sauce of your choice (option)
2 cups stock or clam juice
1/4 cup chopped scallion for garnish

In a heavy Dutch pan with oil and flour, cook, using the wire whisk and stir vigorously until lightly brown, add onion first, take a little time here before toss in the rest ingredients, and the other half of spice. Bring to boil, cover, and cook about 8-10 minutes. Put in prepared shrimp at the last three minutes; adjust the seasoning with of hot sauce. Garnish with scallion.

Yard Long Beans and Shrimp
This bean has a nutty and sweet flavor, good for stir-fry, stew or curry.

1-2 lbs of yard long bean, cut into 2 inches
1lb of med to large shrimp

Spices for shrimp
1/2 t salt and pepper
1t sugar
1T garlic oil or vegetable oil
1T cornstarch

In a medium bowl mix shrimp with spices and oil, set aside.

Aromatic and sauce
1 medium onion sliced
2T-crushed garlic
1T oyster sauce
2T soy sauce
1/2 cup broth

In a large stockpot with sufficient boiling water blanch beans for 6 minutes.

In a wok with high heat and 2T oil put in garlic, this step takes about 20 seconds, add your shrimp, when shrimp loosen up and start to change color, toss in onion and stir fry for 3 to 4 minutes more. By now, bean is ready to drain and add to skillet with shrimp. Pour in sauce, stir well. When everything boil again, turn heat off. Cover; let it rest for a minute or two and dinner are ready to serve.

The Happy Diamond

These rare diamonds come in pairs, and they fit flawlessly together like two happy peas in one merry pod, and they were made for a cheery poster.

I vividly recalled the very first time I appeared at the Bar Harbor Market, I didn't even have a table set up. I was sharing a corner with a vendor selling sandwiches and salad. I don't think this customer knows this information but I'll always remember him as my very first customer at that market. After that first day his wife was usually by his side if she doesn't have to work on Sundays.

There is something peculiar about my memory; I'm not all that good with names. To make up for that I remember faces and his happy outlook leaves an imprint in my head.

This couple attends every Sunday market minus the times when they are traveling around the world. I receive post cards from everywhere their feet touch.

I wish I didn't have to confess this information but here goes, I'm not capable of being chirpy. If something's bothering me I show it, except when I'm at the market I regularly put on a smile because let's face it, that's business. More often than not I fool everyone. Everyone except this special friend of mine; just one look he knows.

Strange things happen when you are surrounded by up-lifting people. You'll fly with them, and their happiness rubs off. I can feel the radiance and see the saturated love between these two. You can see that the everyday affair, the routine along the way, hasn't caused them to lose the passion they feel for each other. I would like to express my sincere appreciation toward the friendship they have happily granted me over all these years. For the laughter every Sunday morning, for always coming back to my table and praising my work.

Thank you for being my happy diamonds.

Happy Shrimp in Creamy Tofu Sauce

Here tofu shows its power as a base for a creamy sauce. I'd be happy any day with this dish. Light and totally delicious!

Shrimp
1lb of large shrimp, shelled, deveined
2t corn starch
1/2t each salt, pepper and cayenne pepper
Mixed shrimp with corn starch, salt, pepper and cayenne pepper

Aromatic
2T crushed garlic
2T fresh grated ginger
8oz ground pork
2t sugar
4T fermented red peppers paste*
1 block of silken tofu, drained.

Sauce
1/2 cup of stock or clam juice
2T oyster sauce
2T light soy sauce
1T fish sauce

Vegetables
4 cups broccoli florets blanched in boiling water for two minutes, scallions for garnish.

In a large skillet with high heat and a thin layer of oil, sauté garlic until fragrant but not brown, add shrimp and stir fry until aromatic, but not cooked through.

Remove shrimp to its original bowl

Back to the skillet with ginger and ground pork, add a bit more oil if needed, cook until pork a bit brown at the edge, then, put in the sugar and let it caramelize.

Next, into the wok are the fermented red pepper paste, tofu and sauce.

With a wooden spoon, stir, as the sauce start to bubbling, this motion will break up tofu; reenter shrimp into skillet, when it starts to boil again toss in broccoli.

Cook until broccoli heated through; scatter in the scallion and serve it right away for best result. This dish goes well with mashed potatoes.

*The fermented pepper paste can be found at any Asian market, this product is either Japanese or Korean.

If you can't find it, substitute with the Thai red pepper paste and cut the amount in half.

For the Love of Pork

The Tale of an Apprentice and Her Sensei

Once upon a time, in the faraway land of Vietnam, they met at the Pilot's club inside Bien Hoa air base, located a little distance from Saigon city.

The apprentice then was young, fresh blood to enter the new game of the black market. The sensei was a bit older and she was on the top of her game. The sensei saw that the potential was there. So without hesitation she took on the task of training the newbie. Not only did they become best friends quickly, they were successfully running an unlawful business. Making profits and having the time of their life were running hand in hand.

What better adventure for two best friends to appear at a Bien Hoa base celebration, than get transported by a helicopter to Saigon Tan- Son- Nhat air base, all in the same night just to go to another party?

The sensei knows everybody, and when she had to deal with a stranger she would use the best weapon on earth: the greens. Who said money can't buy everything? In this case they were wrong.

She taught the apprentice that when you're breaking the law if it fits humble yourself and play ignorant, in a relationship put yourself on the pedestal, if you wait for your man to do it for you, you just might wait until your last breath!

One sad day, the sensei showed up at her apprentice's door in the back seat of a military vehicle, amidst three men in uniform. That's was the last time they saw each other.

The apprentice hired an investigator to locate her best friend, a futile attempt!

Until this day, the apprentice lives with the wisdom from her sensei left behind.

Pork, Eggplant and Lily

The time frame of this story is 1968 in Bien Hoa Vietnam.

My best friend Lily and I attended a concert inside the officer's club, a performance by a Philippine band. We sat right in the front, so of course we were flirting with the band. I guess it paid off, because by the time the music ended for the night we get invited to lunch by the band singer and drummer.

The invitation was for two days later at their house in Saigon. Lily really didn't want to participate. I, however, was thinking with my stomach, so I said,

"Lily, you're just being lazy! It's free food for Christ's sake. Besides, we are going to be in Saigon any way". I could always talk her into mischievous adventures and for most part it usually paid off. This adventure was an interesting one to say the least.

I designated the drummer as her date so I would be the guest of the singer. She did her famous eye roll and sneered, "Whatever!" So, we both got dolled up and arrived at their big house the mid-morning that following Sunday.

They were having a loud party in the middle of the day. I noticed at least three or four bands lived under the same roof, and everybody was strangely happy. Then I spotted out my supposed date, the singer. He doesn't look anything like the one I'd seen two nights ago under concert lights. But he was very courteous and sweet and when he reached out and kissed my hand to my horror I saw all kind of needle marks which spreading all over his fore arms, veins, and wrists. I excused myself, yanked Lily's hand, pulled her to the corner of the room and whispered "Lily, we got to get out, these people are on drugs, let's go."

Lily had the chance of a life time to come down on me and she did it like a hard summer rain in Bien-Hoa. Her lips perched as she smugly said, "Aha! You are the one who insisted to come here now, you are the one who wants to run; I hope you learned something today."

"You sound just like my mother, Lily" I can see out of the corner of my eyes she tried not to break a smile and kept the 'I told you so' attitude.

Then the housekeeper hauled out tons of food and laid it on the long table. My eyes popped, I didn't have to think twice before I heard my own voice declare, "After we eat!"

"Oh Lord, here we go again" she moaned, but moved swiftly to join me at the buffet.

"Oh please, you can't fool me Lilly, you want it as much as I do!" I sneered.

I know she was sharing my thrill at that moment; we've been in the cloak-and-dagger situations before but this one was just fun. I can't say the same for our needle point practitioners as hosts. As much as I want to avoid staring at his wrists, I beginning to search for how many more of them surrounded me. Sadly, I don't have to look very far.

Everything was very well prepared, one particular dish of eggplant grabbed my attention, the pork pieces were slightly spicy and the eggplant was sweet and tender with a bit of tang; right up the alley of my lust for food. After we consumed enough food to make our pain and suffering worthwhile, meaning we reached the point where we couldn't eat anymore, we slipped out, hailed a Taxicab and laughed all the way to the movie theater.

That same band played again the following week. Guess who was missing in the audience? I can't remember the band's name, but I'll forever remember the eggplant dish Lily and I shared that Sunday afternoon.

Eggplant and Spicy Pork
Heat oven to 350 degree

Meat
2lb boneless pork ribs cut into 2x 3 rectangular ½ inch thick
1t salt
1t black pepper
2t cornstarch
Cayenne pepper to your taste

In a medium bowl mixed well, set aside

For the aromatic and vegetables
1 bulb garlic minced
1-2 t hot pepper flakes
1 large red bell pepper, diced
2 medium egg plant cut into large cubes 1 and 1/2lb.
2 cup cherry tomatoes or 1can diced tomatoes

Sauce
1cup broth
2t sugar
1T white vinegar
2, 3T fish sauce
1/2-cup Thai basil
2 slices of bacon

In a large skillet cook the bacon until crispy, remove bacon, leave in the drip, add pork pieces and cook until lightly brown, push all pork to the out-skirt of pan.

Scatter garlic in pan with hot pepper flakes cook about 30 seconds, be careful, do not burn the garlic, bell peppers is the next to go in, then the toma-toes and the sauce, bring all to boil. Arrange egg plant into the sauce, toss to coat it well and put in oven for 30 minutes. Remove, scatter in Thai basil on top with bacon bits and serve at once.

Steam rice is all you need; serves 4 to 6.

Say Hello to Your New Best Friend

July, 1977 I just moved away from Long Beach California and made my new home in Maine in a town called Corinna. There wasn't one Vietnamese person near or far that I knew. Yes, I was digging around for someone to complain with me about the cold and harsh elements of Maine. I looked left and right and nothing and no one came up.

After I settled in, I had to apply for a driver's license and the nearest place was in Dover Foxcroft. As I started the process, the officer who helped with the routine paper work was kind of puzzled at my name (after 30 plus years people still are) and questioned me about it. Jokingly I said, "I'm Vietnamese. I bet you don't see too many faces like mine around here"

"As matter of fact," he cheerfully said, "I do know a very nice lady who lives a block down the road from here. She has been helping other Vietnamese people with their licenses and that's how I know her." I couldn't believe my good fortune.

Quickly I requested if I could have her name and address and he gave it to me without hesitation. I told my husband to take me to her house, he thought I was crazy- nothing new- I suppose. We came upon a nice house nested cozily around the corner of Main Street. I walked up to the outside kitchen door and knocked because I figured all Vietnamese women usually hang out where the food is located, and I was right!

There she was, a tiny woman (most Vietnamese women are, minus me I'm so lucky-not!) She was a bit older than me, just one look at her I knew we would be getting along fabulously. I extended my hand and said

"Hello! I just moved here from California and I'm going to be your new best friend".

See how easy it is? She welcomed me into the lemony colored kitchen and brought out a pot of hot jasmine tea and a platter of cookies. How did she know I loved to eat? This woman was truly a genius. I got just what I wished for and so much more. She enriches my life in so many ways!

Over the course of thirty some years we survived raising kids, sharing domestic headaches and annoying husbands. Hers passed away years ago. Until this day, I'm thankful she's my friend and my confidant because I can tell her just about anything. She would never judge me for all the jasmine tea that comes out of our old country.

I dedicated this dish to my dear friend because it reflected our friendship. It's a Vietnamese classic and no matter how many clever ways I can come up with pork (and I always will) this particular dish remains one of my favorites!

Survivor Pork

Please, follow the directions carefully and don't be fooled by the simplicity of this dish. I've messed it up before and the result was less than perfect (and that always makes me very disappointed). The original version forever called for fatty fresh pork belly, we don't have anything unhealthy in this book. I'm strictly against it!

Prepare 6 hard boiled eggs, set aside.
About 3lbs or a bit more of boneless pork ribs- or butt -cut into a large chunk 2 inches
1/4 cup shallots, smashed with a large knife
1/4 cup fish sauce

In a Dutch pan, mix the pork with shallot and fish sauce; let's rest for 1/2 of an hour
Start with high heat, bring the above mixture to a boiling point; and cook for about five minutes. Pour in 2 cups of coconut soda or 7up. Bring it to boil again; adding hard boil eggs then lower heat to medium and continuous simmer for 30 minutes. The last five minutes, prepare the final sauce.

2T sugar
2t dark soy sauce

In a small sauce pan, caramelize the sugar until golden brown and watch it like a hawk. Soon as it reaches the desired color, ladder some sauce from the simmering pork (about a cup) to the caramelizing pan. Be very careful here, because it'll be bubble big time, stir constantly until sauce is reduced by 50% then add the black soy sauce. Stir, scrape sauce into pork, gently (because of the eggs) mix it all in and cook for another 15 minutes. Remove from heat, stir in 2t coarsely grind black peppers.
 Serve with rice and steamed vegetables.
 Other side dishes that would get along very well with this dish are pickled vegetables or cucumbers with herbs and nuts.
 * Coconut soda usually available at Asian's supermarket.

The Mistake
 Sometimes, I just can't help but believe that there are some things extraordinary I cannot explain, but always marvel when they happen.
 Throughout the history of me doing the markets, I have never made a dish that I didn't sell until one day all that changed.
 It was a very busy day; I sold everything on the table except this one dish. Nobody wanted it. No one even wanted to taste it, as if the dish did not even exist. So, with disappointment I hauled it home and said to myself "damn, I am ending up with this entire sugary dessert!"

I couldn't even eat two bites out of that dessert; instead of sugar I accidentally flavored it with salt. To this day, I still don't know how everybody else knew.

Tenderloin Pork with Grape Tomatoes and Curry Sauce
The sauce that belongs with this dish also happened by mistake. But it was a lovely one!

2 pork tenderloin, about 3lbs

Paste
2t salt
1t each black pepper and brown sugar
1T ancho chili powder
1 garlic bulbs, crushed
2T vegetable oil

Whisk paste and rub it well over meat. This step can be done a day ahead.

Sauce
1 pint sweet grape tomatoes
1T crushed fresh ginger
1T of yellow curry
2T sugar
2T vinegar
Salt to taste

Heat oven to 375 degree
In a large skillet with high heat and just enough oil to coat pan, sear pork until lightly brown and aromatic. Remove meat to a roasting pan, place pan in heated oven and cook until juice runs clear, 20 to 25 minutes.

Tackle the sauce while pork is in the oven. Using the same skillet, adding a bit more oil only if needed. With medium heat, sauté ginger with curry until fragrance before toss in tomatoes, move it around until the tomato skins blister, this step only takes about 2 to 3 minutes, seasoning it with sugar, vinegar and salt to suit your taste. Cover, lower heat and simmer about 2 minutes.

Remove meat from oven, lets it rest a few minutes before you slice and arrange it in a serving platter. Pour sauce over meat, garnish with cilantro only if you like the herb. Believe me; green scallions will do the job just fine and dandy. Serve it with steamed vegetables, rice or noodles for a complete meal!

The Other Stud Muffin from Stonington

Bob Bowen is the other one.

Men like him and women love him. That's the kind of curse my friend Bob has to endure. We have known each other since my very first day of doing markets. Bob welcomed me to the Buck Street place with open arms and later in Bar Harbor and Stonington.

I have to confess that I only tolerated Bob at the beginning and wasn't quite sure how I wanted to deal with someone with such a strong personality, a trait much like mine. It wasn't his fault and I knew where he was coming from considering it's not a fun time putting up with me either. However, Bob is hilarious! He can easily crack a smile out of me in my darkest mood. I wish I could say I return the favor but that would be untrue. I'm not capable of putting on a lighthearted surface smile when I'm upset! Bob can!

Starting in June through the end of September we share three markets a week. Bob has said that sometimes he sees more of me than his own wife. It's sad but I believe him.

There are things we do not see eye to eye on but one thing we both agree on is that during the summer months, the only social life we have is the one at the market.

It's has been a long road and Bob and I have travelled it together. But after this journey one thing is certain: I definitely like the Bob now, a lot more than the Bob I knew at Buck Street. Times are good for him. It seems he's much kinder now. I wish I could say the same for myself but I know it will not be whole truth.

One thing I can say and will stand behind my words. Some of my most memorable meals started with the meat that came from Bob's cooler. When we start going into a slower mode; when he can't pick those heavy coolers up (or maybe he doesn't want to any more) and when I'm not capable of getting up at two o'clock in the morning to stir and to mix, we both may retire. Until then, I would like to thank Bob for his wonderful friendship and encouragement leading me to where I am today

Luscious Chops in Black Bean Sauce

I'm not big with meat but I have to say God help me if I stare into Bob's cooler and spot a piece of pork chop with marble rings because I cannot resist the temptation. Since childhood I have so many good memories associated with this item. Thick or thin, it doesn't matter and I will forever try to cook it in a different ways. Sometimes due to laziness I just rub it with varieties of spices and throw it in the frying pan. That often flies because my husband doesn't care how I cook it as long as he get his meat. This is one technique in my chop's repertoire. Of course it'll never have the power to replace my nanny's dish (from the first book) nonetheless this is a good recipe.

4 medium to thick pork chops

Paste
4 scallions, white part only (reserved the green part for garnish)
1T crushed ginger
1T garlic oil or vegetable oil
1/4t each salt and black pepper

Smash the white part of scallion and mixed in with the rest of the ingredients, rub chops evenly with spices mixture, let it rest for 1 hour, or to overnight.

Sauce
2T rice wine or brandy-option-
2T brown sugar
1/2 cup broth or water
*2t black bean paste
1T soy sauce
1t sesame oil

In a heavy bottom skillet with a light coat of oil and medium high heat cook chop until juice running clear. Remove meat to a serving plate.

Swirl in wine-if use- then brown sugar, broth, bean paste and soy sauce, lower heat scrapping bottom pan to loosen all that gooey and tasty brown stuff let it simmer for 2-3 minutes, sauce shouldn't be runny. Taste it, sauce should be a bit on the salty side, savory and lightly sweet, the wine giving a good lift to the aroma here. Add sesame oil and chopped green scallion.

Remove sauce from heat, and then pour it over meat.

*I preferred the Korean black bean paste; look for it at your local gourmet food store.

The paste itself very salty, use it cautiously, it easier to add more if needed.

A Pâté for All Occasions
Don't be intimidated by the word pâté, it's nothing but a fancy meat loaf. I designed this recipe without liver. But if you don't mind that stuff simply add a half (½) of cup of coarsely chopped chicken liver to the final step (before you put it in the oven).

3/4 cup of Cognac or Brandy

In a small sauce pan boil it down to1/4 of a cup, let cool.

1/2 cup of shallots, sliced, sauté with 2T spoon of butter until fragrant, set aside.

Whole pork tenderloin (about 19 to 20 ounces) sliced, toss with the prepared alcohol and put it in the refrigerator for 20 minutes.

1lb of good bacon, prefer low salt and not too fatty. Divided, coarsely chopped about 8ounces. Reserve the rest for final step.

1t salt
1/2t sugar
1T coarsely grind black pepper
1 egg
1/4 cup heavy cream

Preheat oven to 350 degree.

With a loaf pan, lay 4- 5 slice of bacon down. In food processor pulse pork mixture, important not to make it mush (just coarse) add shallots, salt, pepper, egg and cream. Pulse a few more times, fold in the chopped bacon, and scrape all of it into prepared loaf pan. Lay the rest of bacon on top. Place loaf pan in a bigger pan, and fill the outside of loaf pan to half way with boiling water, then carefully place the whole thing in oven.

Bake in preheated oven for 1hour and half. Let it cool off; serve it with crackers or French Baguette

Bird Nest Pâté and Egg

Here is a good breakfast using the left over pâté.

1/2 cup of quick cooking grits
2 cups boiling water
1/2t salt
1 thick slice of pate, coarsely chopped
2 eggs
Salt and peppers to taste

In a microwaveable bowl cook grits with high power for five minutes.

In a nonstick skillet, lightly brown Pate, separate into two parts, form it into two round rings, crack each ring with an egg. Cook egg to your desired doneness, over easy or sunny side up, add salt and pepper.

Remove grits from microwave oven, divide into two serving dishes, lay the bird nest Pate and egg on top. Serve (2)

The Lost Meatballs

There is the place called NhaTrang located at the central region of Vietnam coast and this place is nationally famous for its meatballs. I have an aunt who lives there. She's pretty and she married into an extremely wealthy family. I've never met her but I take my mother's word simply because that's the way it is in any culture, particularly from Vietnam, no unattractive woman I know marries a rich man. So, of course growing up I often fantasized what it was like to live in her shoes with servants and a mansion. I wished that I could at least visit them so I could eat all the meat balls to my little heart's desire. Then, one day, my aunt had to give up all those privileges and runaway because she loathed her mother-in-law so much. I totally understand why she had to run away from all that drama. I never got the chance to eat all those meatballs.

The Found Meat Balls

For this dish, I cut down on the work without sacrificing the taste that makes this dish special. An authentic technique, maybe not, but an authentic taste, absolutely.

Meat

1 1/2 to 2 lbs of pork loin, trimmed off all excess fat around it and sliced thin
1/2 cup shallot, sliced thin
1/4 cup garlic, sliced thin
2T fish sauce (no substitute here)
2t of sugar
1t freshly ground black pepper
2T potatoes starch
2 ounces of pork fat, minced
1T each shallot oil and garlic oil (only if you don't use the pork fat)

In the medium bowl combine all the ingredients above (minus the pork fat if use) mixed well, marinate and chill in the freezer for 30 minutes.

With food processor run with high speed, process this partially frozen meat until it turn into a smooth paste, don't over load, you are not going to get a good result if you do. Paste should be sticky and spring back to your touch. At this point enter the pork fat (if use) just pulse enough to combine, very important not to turn paste into mush. Scrape this mixture into a greased bowl.

Rub a little oil into the palm of your hand and grab a hand full of meat then squeeze out between your index and thumb finger, keep rolling meat around with this motion until its form a smooth ball, scoop out the meat ball with an oiled spoon, and lay all down to a nonstick baking tray. Repeat until all paste is used.

The meat balls can be threaded onto soaked bamboo skewers – I prefer the stainless steel one-You'll need at least 12, grill it over charcoal fire. Turn meat frequent so they get to cook through evenly.

Talking about slavery for meat balls! If you are thinking the work stops here, think again.

To serve these found meat balls you'll need the following ingredients

1 platter of vegetables with lettuce, bean sprouts thinly sliced cucumber, mint and cilantro for herb.
1 package of rice paper 16oz
1 package of rice noodles 16oz
Spicy peanut dipping sauce

Prepare the vegetables ahead, can be done the day before, cook the rice noodles in boiling water for five minutes, drain, rinse with cold water, make the dipping sauce.

Sauce
1 cup of chicken broth
2T tomatoes paste
1/3 cup of creamy peanut butter
1/4 cup hoisin sauce
1-3T chili garlic paste (can be find at grocery store)
*2T sugar
2T vinegar
2T garlic oil

In food processor mixed all ingredients until smooth. May be served with extra roasted chopped peanuts and hot peppers sliced.

To ensemble
Dip rice paper into warm water; lay it down, put in a piece of lettuce, cucumber, rice noodles, herbs and meat ball. Roll it up tightly and dip it into your own small bowl of dipping sauce.

A good party dish, just lay everything out and let your guest do the rolling.

*You might need to adjust the amount of sugar; depending on how much chili garlic paste is used.

The Zero Heroes
"Is there any sugar in this dish?" I looked up and saw a lady with a bright hair color.

"The most would be a teaspoon per serving of 16oz," I said.

"I guessed I have to pass, I'm trying to cut down on the sugar" she shook her head and sauntered off toward the front door exit.

I love sugar and at times I'll give in to my evil side and have something sweet and other times I wouldn't even think twice about it. But this woman was so strict; she wouldn't even give in to one teaspoon. Wow! I was so impressed. She was my hero at that moment. Sadly, it lasted no more than five minutes because she makes a stop at the Greek's vendor down the aisle and buys a platter of baklava, picks one up and whoops it down in seconds. Then to my horror she popped another one in her mouth while she's paying for it.

Sweet and Succulent Spare Rib Nuggets

Put your sugar in here for a good cause.

1 small rack of spare ribs (3 to 4lbs) trim the fat, separated and cut into 1 and ½ inch nuggets. Blot dry well with paper towel.
1/4 cup brown sugar
1 cup of broth
2 T light soy sauce
1 T dark soy sauce
1 large sweet onion, cubes
1 bulb garlic, peeled crushed
1 each red and yellow bell pepper, cubed
1 bunch of scallions, cut into 2 inch pieces

In wok, or heavy bottom skillet with 1T oil brown rib nuggets, use high heat, and don't let ribs pile on top of each other.

To prevent it from creating too much moisture, you might want to do it in two batches. When ribs all nicely brown, scatter sugar around the outskirt of pan, and then slowly blend it into rib. As the sugar starts to caramelize add garlic and watch it like a hawk, you only have to spend 10 to 15 seconds here, have the broth close by, pour it in soon as you can detect garlic aroma, bring it to boil then cover, lower heat and simmer for half an hour.

Open, turn heat up to high again then add onion, stir it around for couple of minutes, next to go in is the soy sauce then bell pepper. Now, you are the one calling the shots here, up to you to decide if you want your pepper tender or crispy, it can go on for 1 or 5 minutes. Remove from heat, turn in the scallion and freshly ground black pepper and get ready to enjoy your sugar.

The Love from Bar Harbor

I can't remember one opening day in Bar Harbor when there was decent weather. It was always cold, wet, and windy.

Just a few of us would show up on really crappy days: Bob with meat, Matt with flowers, Becky with bread, Jordan with goat's milk products, and me. I have never missed the opening simply because I know there will be people coming to see me and vice versa. I can't wait to see them either (despite the fact that I know it wouldn't be much of a day as far as business is concerned). To me, getting more acquainted with the people taking time to visit me week after week is far more important than business. There is a time slot in May (and maybe early June) that I am able to do that. In July my line is long that for the most part business affairs must be conducted and it's very hard to find time to chat with my favorite customers. The groups of people who show up at the first market are diehard fans. They are not just customers, they are our friends.

One opening day she walked toward my table with a bouquet of flowers, long red hair flying because of the crazy wind. She said she was happy to see me, we hugged, and we talked. Our conversation made it seem like the six month absence didn't even happen. After picking up her favorite dishes she said she would see me next week and sauntered off. She might be gone now but her presence lingered on with scent of the bouquet she left for me.

For the Love of Ribs with Honey
To say I love this dish is an understatement; it is one dish with many uses. Toss it into a salad or slice and pile it inside French bread for a great sandwich. It'll turn a package of instant noodles soup into something special and it'll freeze well.

Meat

3lbs of country boneless rib, cut length wise into 2 Inch thick strips

Marinade
1 bulb of garlic crushed
1/2 cup of broth
1/3 cup of honey
1 and 1/2 t salt
2T light soy sauce
1T dark soy sauce
3T rice wine
2T tomato paste
1t five spices powder
2t sesame oil

In a large bowl, mixed marinade and toss in pork. Cover and refrigerate from 2hr to 24hr. Heat oven to 450 degree. Drain and reserve marinade for later use.

You might roast it on top of oven rack, over a deep pan with a couple of inches of hot water to catch the drips.

Sometimes, when I'm not quite motivated, I just lay them separated in a large roasting pan. Bake them in hot oven for 25 minutes then lower heat to 350 for another 20 minutes longer, baste and turn frequently the last ten minutes.

With the first option you will get a better result.

The Comedian

If I said Andy Smith was a funny man then I wouldn't be saying the whole truth! He and his wife Libby own and operate Smith's smoke house from Monroe. Their business is very well known by folks who can't live without jerky, smoked cheese, smoked salmon, bacon and the best ham you can sink your teeth into. I can vouch for that!

We go way back Andy and me. There was a time at the Buck Street market where the space was so tight that we were next to each other and squished under each other's arm pits. For that reason Andy obtained lots of information (or ammunition) from observing me at work. In time he became very good at mimicking my accent and having one hell of a good time doing it. I have to admit he's a pro at this job but he's much better when he has a side kick: my daughter.

Customers at the market know Samantha but what they might not know is Sam is totally hilarious and just like Andy; she also loves to poke fun of me. Lucky for Andy she has twenty years plus watching me at home.

Something devastating happens to me when both of them team up: they turned themselves into a dynamic comedian duo. They feed off each other with endless material and I can't defend myself because I always start laughing until every organ inside of me begs me to stop. I always hope for a busy day in Bar Harbor because, give us a slow day and all I have to do is look up and see Andy leaving his table heading to ours. Then I know what will come up next.

The roasting Bich Nga show is about to start!

At first Andy was only doing the Buck street market in the winter; of course he has bigger fish to fry during the summer months. He was the one who pointed it out that I would do a lot better in Orono.

I thought about Andy's advice for a long time but I never took any action to move.

The summer my first book came out I applied to join the Orono market and the rest is just history. I have my friend Andy to thank for that sleek transition. So Andy can make fun of me anytime he chooses and he'll still get my blessing.

Funny Pork with Tequila and Limejuice

This peculiar dish has Andy's character written all over: sweet, tangy, spicy, sort of one of a kind special. Beware: you might get hooked!

Meat
2lbs of boneless rib cut into 1 inch cubes
1/2t each salt and black pepper
2t good quality chili powder
2t anato powder
1t ground cumin
1T red-hot pretty oil or olive oil

In a large bowl with the above ingredients, mix until well blend

Spices and sauce
Zest of one lime, reserve the juice.
1 garlic bulb peeled, crushed
2T sugar
1/4 cup Tequilla
1/4 cup soy sauce
Cilantro, chopped Jalapeno peppers for garnish.

In a large skillet with high heat and a thin layer of oil, sear pork pieces. Make it two batches so it'll brown nicely, scatter in sugar, garlic and lime zest, take a little time here then add Tequilla. Let the alcohol do its duty then add soy sauce, cover and cook for 5 minutes, open it up, stir, make sure sauce is coated evenly.

Remove from heat before adding cilantro and Jalapeno pepper. Serve it with Spanish rice or wrap it up inside a tortilla with grated cheese.

The Secret Affair
She was one of my diamonds from the early days at the Buck Street market. She was tall, trim and fabulously fit. She liked to work out and it showed. I wished I could feel that way! For me, working out is another form of paying dues. I do it because I'm cheap and I would hate to go shopping for jeans in the next size up.

Like clockwork, she always showed up early and only purchased the small 8oz containers of several items. Five (to be exact) small containers for every lunch she had at work and then egg rolls for snacks in between.

One Saturday morning, all that had changed.

"Double size up of everything, please!" she said it impatiently

"Why?" I asked

She slams a bag of larger containers down (she always brought her own).

"My freaking husband discovered my secret affair that's why."

"You had an affair?"

"He found the stashes of your food in the back of the refrigerator, while I was away visiting my mom in the hospital. He must have liked everything because there was nothing left for me to take to work for lunch all week long. I'm so angry! So guess what? Now I have to share and I don't want to."

I couldn't help but laugh along with the people around us. I dished out all of her favorites and when it came to the stir fry chicken dish she requested triple in size, shaking her head.

"He asked for that dish, if I don't get enough he will get his paws all over mine."

I handed her the bag. She made a groaning sound once she heard the amount of the new bill. I snickered.

"Chalk it up and pay for your sins, lady! Every affair has a price tag. This is a bargain!

She loves everything that's stuffed especially stuffed tomatoes with pork. The farmer's market is the place you can find a variety of tomatoes. I usually have this dish on the menu by late July and it always sells out quickly. The different choices of colors used to make this dish are absolutely stunning to look at, but the taste is what makes customers come back for more.

Choose slightly under ripe tomatoes for easier handling.

Stuffed Tomatoes with Pork

8 medium size tomatoes, slightly under ripe, cut about an inch from the top; scoop the inside out, reserved. Dust inside tomatoes with cornstarch, set aside.

Stuffing

In a large mixing bowl, combine and mix until it well blended

2lbs ground pork
2 oz of bean thread soaked for 15 minutes, drained, chopped.
1/2 cup chopped sweet onion
1/2t each salt and pepper
1t sugar
2T fish sauce
1T garlic oil

Stuff filling into prepared tomatoes

Sauce
2T minced garlic
1cup of broth
The reserved tomatoes, chopped
Salt, sugar as needed

Bunch of scallion cut into 2inches
Cilantro for garnish

Cook

In a large skillet with a thin coat of oil brown the meat side of the stuffed tomatoes, scatter in the garlic, stir until garlic gives out its aroma then, pour in the sauce, make the executive decision here about salt and sugar, and bring it to boil. Cover, lower heat to simmer for 1/2 an hour. Remove from heat before adding herbs.

Wide egg noodles would be a nice choice for side kick; you can't go wrong with rice either.

Stuffed Cabbages with Chicken and Pork

Every now and then I'll feature this item at the market. It takes a bit of work. Well, maybe a little more than a bit, but I need my fix too. So what choice do I have? As if I can go into the grocery store and buy it. There is no way out for me.

Filling
8oz boneless chicken breast, minced
8oz ground pork
1/2 cup finely chopped sweet onion
2T finely chopped garlic
1t each salt pepper and sugar
1T fish sauce or soy sauce
1/4 cup chopped cilantro
1T corn starch, potatoes starch or arrow root powder

In a large mixing bowl combine all the above ingredients and mix it well, set it aside while prepping the vegetables and sauce.

*Cabbage for stuffing
12 large outer leaves of cabbage
Equal amount of scallion stalks

Blanch cabbage leaves in boiling water for 2 minutes do the same for scallions for 15 seconds.

Sauce
2T vegetables oil
4 large ripe tomatoes, diced.
1/4 cup shallot, minced

Salt and sugar to taste
1cup chicken or vegetable stock

To trim off the tough stem; hold on to the base of leaf with your left hand and glide the tip of a sharp knife- starting with the lower tough end- cut it away from you.

To stuff
Lay all trimmed cabbage leaves down, divide meat equally over them; roll them up like you are rolling egg rolls, then secure each with a stalk of blanched scallion.

Cook
In a large skillet with high heat swirl in oil, let it get a bit smoky and sauté the shallot until lightly brown at the edge before adding tomatoes, pour in stock, sugar and salt to your desired taste. When it starts to a good boil, situate rolls over sauce, make a little room in between and cover. Cook for 30 minutes in boiling sauce. Rolls are done when they're nicely glazed with sauce and not runny. Freshly ground black pepper is all you need for a finishing touch.
    *Spring or summer cabbage is an ideal for this dish.

Stuffed Sweet Onions with Spicy Pork
You'll need to use the food processor for this task. Otherwise, you'll be tied to the chopping board until the cows come home.

Onions
2 large sweet onions, such as Vidalia, peel and remove skin. Cut each length wise in half, scoop out about 2 table spoons to create a pocket. Reserve it for later use.

Filling
1 medium size red bell pepper, charred, peeled
2 Jalapeno peppers, charred, peeled
1lb pork loin, sliced
1egg white
1/2t each salt, black pepper and quality chili powder
1t sugar
1T tapioca powder
2T fish sauce or 2T light soy sauce
1t sesame oil only if you chose to use soy sauce
1T shallot oil if using fish sauce

Put all stuffing ingredients along with the scooped out onion in the food processor, and pulse on and off until everything is coarsely chopped.

Divide filling evenly into four onion cups. Bake in 375 degrees oven for 1 hour. Glaze it with roasted garlic and hot pepper jam for a beautiful final touch However; it's optional in your part. My customer will always get it with the whole nine yards.

Serves 2 as a main course or 4 as an appetizer

Tofu

Here, I'll enter a chapter with a mixed feeling. Either you love it or hate it!

I'm not here to advocate for soy or endorse tofu for your health.

I need to say tofu is very important for me and (my customers). For that reason you'll find tofu at my table throughout the market season. But to make sure you are able to bring some home, you have to show up early. What's that tell you?

A large non-stick skillet is the must-have tool to tackle tofu. It helps to brown and that's the first step for most dishes belonging in this category.

Always dry tofu thoroughly and season it well before you cook.

Use firm tofu for all-purpose

Extra firm is good for the grill

Soft is suitable for soup

The silken tofu type is appropriate for dessert or as base for sauce and dip.

The Last Sunday

I spotted her smile from the corner of the street long before I had to take my left turn to enter my parking space at Bar Harbor market.

More often than not I see her with a basket in her hand, standing patiently and waiting for me. She usually carried her own containers.

She would try any tofu dish I made. I doubt it if she even knew what tofu was before we met. This is how she would praise our relationship.

"We have a really good thing going on here between you and me. As long as you keep on cooking, I'll keep on eating." That is always music to my ears.

Then, one Sunday afternoon, she showed up unusually late. A long time friend had flown in from out of town and she wanted us to meet.

We always hug, this time she was trembling. She had recently gotten the news that she had a tumor.

We visited for some time that afternoon. I told her I believed with all my heart she would be okay. Then we said good-bye. I wished I had known that was the last Sunday for the two of us.

The following week, her daughter showed up. She set a sack over the table, tears streaming down her cheeks. I reached out and held her hands, and there was no need for words.

I opened the bag and inside there were a lovely Bar Harbor sweat shirt and a red rain jacket. Until this day I still wear them. And when I do, I can't help but think of her.

Sometimes, when the sun is shining at the right angle, just before I turn into the parking lot, I can still see her smile, with the basket in her hand and waiting for her tofu.

I bet she knows I miss her.

Golden Lady

Talking about seduction! I can eat a lot of these sticks. Make double or triple batches and enjoy it all week long.

1 block of firm tofu cut into 8 sticks
1/2t each salt, pepper and sugar
1T cornstarch
In a large plastic bag, gently shake and mixed them well, set aside. This step can be done day ahead.
2 beaten eggs mixed with 1 T soy sauce
1/2 cup Panko breadcrumb

In a large nonstick skillet with high heat and a thin coat of oil, dip tofu sticks in egg then roll into Panko bread crumbs and brown it on all sides, add bit more oil as needed. Serve with your favorite dipping sauce. This is mine.

Ginger and Miso dipping sauce
1/4 cup soybean Miso
 1/4 cup rice wine vinegar (or white)
*1T light soy sauce
1/4 cup Mirin rice wine
1T grated ginger
1T honey
1T garlic oil or 2t sesame oil

Mixed well, store it inside a glass jar and its will keep for two weeks in refrigerator.
*Depended on the brand of Miso, you might not need soy sauce.
Tips: for more intense taste, a teaspoon of powder mushrooms or tomato powder might be added to the shaking.

Lady and the Golden Beet

I really like the color of golden beets but any beet will do. Go to your local Farmer's Market for a variety.

4 -5 cups of golf ball size golden beets. Wash and steam beets until tender but not mushy about 20 to 30 minutes.

1 block of medium firm tofu cut into cubes

Dressing

In a large bowl mixed well

3T soy sauce
1/4 cup olive oil
1/4 cup balsamic vinegar
1T mince garlic, 3 cloves
1T garlic oil
Hot oil and hot pepper flake (option)

Divide dressing into two parts, cut beet in half, and slice it up or quarter
Toss 1/2 of dressing over beet, mix pour into a deep plate, toss other half with tofu, spoon tofu on top beet and garnish it with 1/4 cup Thai basil or herb of your choice.

The Rose Effect

I lived next door to the Fisher Farm. That's makes Rosie my neighbor but most importantly she's my friend. I'm a lifer at this spot in the town called Winterport. Rosie and her family didn't show up until much later. (So, for the record I'm the senior resident.)

In the earlier days we shared two markets a week. If anyone complimented me about how hard they thought I worked I often said "it was nothing compared to my friend Rosie" and I wouldn't be exaggerating.

The Fisher's own a beautiful farm. I'm green with envy every time I stroll down their land in the summer. But, as much as I'm jealous I know there is no way in this world I could do their job. Just one look at their display of vegetables and flowers at the market

Picture speaks a thousand words.-

Every morning, especially in the summer, I'm out the door to do my routine walk. And every morning there's Rosie already in her garden. She seems to beat me every time.

Years back, not long after I joined the Bar Harbor family, Rosie advised me to give the Northeast market a shot. My initial thought was how am I going to handle all that work? I had my doubts. She encouraged me, "It's only eight weeks, and you'll do well there." She was right! I hopped on the wagon and until this day the ride is still smooth. She knows! Last year Rosie retired. That means she doesn't come to the market any more. But, most of time, when I walk by her house I still see Rosie in the garden putting her imprint into every inch of soil. She's always out there, resilient, that's my friend Rosie!

Lady in Red

Whenever the eggplant is ready to be picked in my garden, you'll see it featured in the menu.

I prefer the slender oriental eggplant for this dish. Where can you find it around here except at your local Farmer's market? In my case, I'm lucky to live next door to my friend Rosie; if my garden fails to give out any eggplant I know exactly where I can find some.

Tofu
2lbs of firm tofu cut into 1inch cubes
1t salt
1/2 t pepper
2T tomato powder

In a plastic bag shake them together. This step can be done ahead.

Vegetables and sauce
2lb baby eggplant or regular eggplant cut into cubes
2T Thai red curry paste
2 cups stock or 1 can of broth
2 cups fresh squeeze coconut cream or 1 can
2T fish sauce
1-2t sugar
For garnish fresh sliced red Jalapeno pepper and Thai basil*

In a large nonstick skillet with a thin coat of oil, brown tofu, shake pan back and forth for better color. After this step, gently move tofu to the outside of pan. Put the red curry paste in the middle and sauté it for about 30 seconds, place eggplant on top, pour in sauce and bring to boil. I don't care for mushy egg plant; so, check it at two or three-minute intervals. Remove from heat, toss in Basil and hot pepper if use.

Red Curry Paste

Nothing wrong with store brought paste unless you are picky like me, then you'll have to make it yourself.

2oz dried, hot or mild Mexican chili.
2t coriander seed

1t shrimp paste (for vegetarian use1T peanut butter)
1/3 cup chopped shallot
1/4cup garlic clove
4 lime kaffir leaves
2 stalks of lemon grass use the white part only. Sliced thin
1 to 3 fresh Thai dragon peppers
2t ginger

Remove the seeds and stems from dried pepper and soak in warm water for ½ hour.

In heavy pan over medium heat toast coriander seed until fragrant, 1 minute, cool off and grind in mortar and pestle (or coffee grinder)

Drain chilies, reserving the liquid. Put all ingredients into food processor, and process, adding just enough reserved liquid to make a moist paste.

Store paste in the refrigerator for 2 weeks or freeze for later use.

My Fifty Cent Sale

We don't always have peaceful weather at the Bar Harbor market. At least a few times each season we get hit with real stormy days. Sometimes the weather is so severe we have to pack up and leave early. If anyone was stubborn enough to stay, the first on the list would be Bob Bowen- the meat man. Second would be me.

This particular day, not only did a torrential rain terrorize us but the wind picked everything up and blew it in every direction. Everybody around me was wrapping up and Bob was the last one in line. After Bob took down his tent he looked over, my space was directly next to his and he noticed that I was not making any effort to pack up. It was very like Bob to say, "Bich Nga's waiting for her fifty cent sale".

I was busy with customers up to that moment. The parking lot was nearly empty even though we still had another hour of market remaining. I still had quite a lot of food on the table. The right thing would have been to call it a day and leave like everyone else, but my sixth sense begged me to stay. It was continuously at odds with my common sense.

I watched Bob's truck pull away from the parking lot. I was all alone now and feeling totally uneasy because of the outlook of no further sales. Five minutes had gone by and nothing happened. I started to doubt my own instincts. I told myself I should wrap it up and leave. Then, all of a sudden I heard the distant sound of an engine. A car approached and the driver drove directly to the front of my table. She stepped out of her car with both hands gripping a large cooler. She said eagerly

"Thank god you're still here! I'm going home today so I have to stock up, am I too late?"

She cleaned out all the food. She got a good deal and so did I. I drove home in the pouring rain plus gushing winds and despite all the water I had wiped off my face from Bar Harbor's terrible storm, I was unable to wipe off the grin across my face.

Lady in Yellow Curry Sauce

Bob loves tofu! I don't think he'd share this information with everybody. He keeps it all wrapped up very well (maybe because everybody knows him as the meat man). Oops, the secret's out. This is one of Bob's favorites.

1 block of firm tofu cut into cubes, toss with 1t each salt and pepper.
2 med size sweet potatoes cut into cubes
2T-minced garlic
1 medium onion cubed
1T yellow quality curry
1/4 cup of (raw) blanched almond. Coarsely ground
2 T sundried tomatoes coarsely chopped
2 bay leaves
1can coconut cream-2cups-
1 can of vegetables broth or 2 cups stock
1-2t salt or to your taste
1t sugar
Cilantro for garnish

In a large and deep non-stick skillet with a thin coat of oil lightly brown the tofu, remove, set aside. Back to skillet with a bit more oil if needed, sauté the onion and garlic until fragrant, add almond, stir, taking a little time here before pouring in broth, coconut and salt. Bring it to boil, arrange tofu in the outer layer, sweet potatoes piled in the middle, sprinkle in dry tomatoes on top, and add the bay leaves. Cover, cook for 10 to 12 minutes. Sweet potatoes should be tender but firm.

Remove from heat before adding herbs.

A loaf of crusty whole grain bread makes a super addition!

Festival Kale

Once a month, the Belfast market would have a street festival. It's a good opportunity to see a whole lot of people who don't usually come to visit us at our regular space. The distance between the two places is only about an eighth of a mile. I will never understand why some people only come to the festival.

In early June fresh vegetables from the garden are out of question, so every year about that time I have to depend on wholesale. The large dish of red kale sautéed in ginger garlic sauce looks amazing so there was no surprise to me that it was moving rather quickly. I tucked a little bit away because I didn't want to go home with an uncertainty of what kind of vegetables to have with dinner.

Once dinner came my husband bit into his kale as I crunched into mine, we looked at each other and said it in unison, "This kale is so bitter."

At that historic moment the phone rang and somebody at the other end was asking if I was going to have that delicious red kale dish (the same one we were dreading to finish) again next week. I didn't have to think at all about the answer—————NO!

Lady in Green
Green curry paste
    1t coriander seed, lightly toasted

1/4t anise
1 lime kaffir leaves
A handful of cilantro
1T ginger
3 cloves garlic
1 small onion
2 Serrano chilies
3 large romaine lettuce leaves
1 T sugar
1/4 cup light soy sauce
In food processor pulse the above ingredients to a green paste, set aside.
2 blocks of firm tofu cut into cubes
About 2, 3 cups cut up vegetables such as bell peppers, string beans or zucchini.
2 cups broth
1 can of coconut milk
1/2 cup Thai basil
Sliced hot pepper to your taste

In a Dutch pan bring broth and paste to a boil; arrange vegetables and tofu in pan cook until vegetables are tender but crisp. Stir in coconut milk and Thai basil, sliced hot pepper if desired. Serve with rice. Serves 4-6

Sunset Sweet Diamond
She is, indeed, my sweetest diamond from Stonington! From the first day we met I felt the connection between us and without any difficulty we became friends.

When my first book was coming out, she hosted a cooking party at her gorgeous home in Sunset with me as a guest chef and a lot of her close friends.

What a fantastic time we had. After a few bottles of wine, we were all hanging loose and letting everything take wing and soar. Laughter, without end that was the part I mostly recall on that special day.

One year at the last market day, she invited me to have lunch with her and I happily agreed. But, at the last minute, I had doubts when I thought about the truck load of work waiting for me when I got home and having lunch would make my getting home much later than usual. I told myself I deserved a break then I ran into another complication: I couldn't find her house. The last time I was there had been two years before. I got deeper and deeper lost and at one point I told myself maybe I should give up, turn around, and go home. I'm so glad I didn't. I was about half an hour late, but I got there. When I walked into her spacious kitchen I faced a beautiful crust-less crab quiche, fresh green salad, and crispy golden French bread. Best of all she was waiting for me with an open arms, happy to see me.

The food was delicious and so was my host, we talked, we laughed and the hour just flowed by. I looking out her window and I could see a sail boat in the distance. A beautiful afternoon by the bay with all the best ingredients made a great memory. At that moment I clearly understood the meaning of "take time to smell the roses". That's how I'll always remember her as my sunset diamond.

She'll always be my biggest fan regarding tofu!

Tofu, Swiss chard, and Shiitake Mushrooms
Tofu
1lb of firm tofu, dried, sliced into 8 pieces
In a medium plastic bag shake tofu slices with:
1T mushroom powder (option)
1T cornstarch
1/2t each salt, black pepper and sugar

Shake until all pieces coat well with seasoning, set aside

Vegetables
A bundle of rainbow Swiss chard, washed, rinsed coarsely chopped. (About 2lbs)
1lb of fresh Shiitake mushrooms trimmed off stems, cut in half

For the aromatic and sauce
1T grated ginger
2T light soy sauce

1t dark soy sauce
1/4 cup sweet wine such as Mirin
1/4 cup vegetable broth
2t sesame seed oil

In a large nonstick skillet with a thin layer of oil, brown tofu pieces evenly over both sides, remove from skillet, set it aside.

Back to skillet with the grated ginger add a bit more oil if needed, sauté ginger with Shiitake mushrooms until fragrant add the greens and cook until greens start to wilt. Flash in the wine, broth and sauce, cover, and cook for about two to three minutes. Open it up, time for the return of the leading lady.

Lay the slices tofu in between the greens and mushrooms let it bubble up for few more minutes add the sesame oil and remove it from heat. Here you have it all plus taste. Serve with rice!

Swiss chard

This item is available from early spring into late fall at the Farmers Market. Look for the crisp stalks and vivid green leaf with no blemish in between. Swiss chard is loaded with important vitamins. Some people called it "the other spinach"

I call it the simply delicious!

The Busy Summer's Day of Bar Harbor

As soon as I drove into the parking lot that Sunday morning in Bar Harbor, I noticed cameramen everywhere setting up tripods. I knew something was going on but what.

Soon enough, the answer came along from one of my customers. A famous lady was in town and all that fuss would pave the way for one of her show segments.

I was busy so I didn't even notice her until she stopped right in the front of my table. She smiled sweetly and said something about Vietnamese food into the camera. I figured she was talking about me, so I looked up and said,

"Well, hello there! Now I know why all the traffic is here today"

She pointed at the stuffed tofu on the table and asked for one. I set it on a serving plate and handed it to her, she gushed as she bite into the triangle

"Tofu with green vegetables, it's so delicious and so nutritious, who would think to come to Maine for this? When you're in Maine you are thinking of lobster."

Well, to make a long story short, before she left the famous lady reminded me to turn on my television the following Thursday to watch her show and left.

I noticed the happy face she wore fell right off after the cameras stopped filming.

Just as she left the scene the conversation started at my line and everything that was said was not all that warm and fuzzy. I had heard enough of the negativity so I put my arms up in the air and said with authority,

"Please give the lady a freaking break! It's not that easy being rich and famous. I wouldn't mind having her bank account but I do not want to walk in her shoes.

Okay, maybe just one day and no, I wouldn't pick the day when she was in jail. Besides, she gives me business every now and then plus she likes my tofu. Unless she lied to the camera! You all witness that, right?"

"She told the truth this time, that tofu dish is the reason I'm here every week," A man said with a grin on his face.

"Same here," A lady standing behind him joined.

I felt the warmth from these responses and that is the reason why I love my job and I couldn't imagine any size bank account that can match that feeling.

Lady in the Black Forest
Tofu
1 block of firm tofu cut into cubes
1 T cornstarch
*2T mushroom powder (option)
1/2 t each, salt, pepper, sugar, onion powder, garlic powder

Put all the ingredients above in the plastic bag, shake well, and set aside. This step can be done a day ahead.

Vegetables and spices
**1 dozen of dried Shiitake mushrooms, soaked until tender. Drained, save the liquid.
5 to 6 small baby Bok Choy heads
2t crushed ginger
2t chili garlic sauce (option)

Sauce
Mushroom liquid or 1cup of stock
2T Mirin wine or rice wine
1T oyster sauce
1T light soy sauce
1T dark soy sauce
Sesame oil as desired
Wash Bok Choy; blanch in boiling water for one minute.

In a large nonstick skillet with just a light coat of oil, brown tofu on all sides if possible,

Remove tofu, back to skillet drizzle in a bit more oil as needed, sauté onion and ginger, put in chili garlic (if use) then mushrooms and tofu, stir in sauce, bring to boil and cook for 3 to 4 minutes so the tofu has a chance to absorb the sauce, adding Bok Choy, cook another minute then remove from heat, add sesame oil.

Toasted, black sesame seed for garnish (option)

*You can buy regular dried white button mushrooms, grind it in coffee mill.

** Small size preferred

To Fry or Not to Fry

Sometimes I crave a piece of fried tofu to dip into a hot and spicy fish sauce or ginger soy with fresh chilies.

Some people might be turned off with the word fry, maybe the fear of the hot oil or the odor. If you know how to fry properly you really can have the cake and eat it too. To do this task you'll need a thermometer. Oil that is not hot enough will create greasy and soggy results, on the other hand, oil too hot will burn the food before it cooks through, this tool will help to make this task simple as a walk in a park!

Fear of hot oil splattering, (or the worst night mare) oil would boil over and ooze all over the stove? No problem, just before adding food into the boiling oil, sprinkle in a little salt.

Lady in Golden Pond
2 blocks of firm tofu cut into cubes
1/4 cup mushroom powder
1T cornstarch
1t each salt and pepper

In a larger bowl or plastic bag, shake it well, set aside

Paste
2 large cloves shallot
3 cloves garlic
2T quality yellow curry powder
2T garlic oil or vegetable oil

In food processor pulse the above ingredients to a golden paste

Vegetables and sauce
3, 4 cups root vegetables such as potatoes, carrot or winter squash cut up
2 cups broth
2 cups coconut milk
Salt to taste, cilantro for garnish

In a Dutch pan, or a nonstick skillet with heavy bottom and a light film of oil, gentle stir fry the paste until fragrant 2, 3 minutes add broth, bring to boil. Arrange vegetables in pan, make a well in the center, gently set in tofu, cover, cook until vegetables are tender, pour in coconut milk, bring it all to a gentle boil then turn the heat off, add salt as needed, sprinkle with cilantro and sliced hot pepper if desired.
 Serve (4 to 6)
Leftovers are more than welcome for this dish.

Rich Man's Lady
 In Vietnam tofu is our year round staple. We don't eat tofu because we are being health conscious; we just don't have any other choice because it fits everyone's budget. Every blue moon, the rich people will bend over to share our bliss. This recipe is the result of that special occasion.

Tofu
 2lbs of firm tofu cut into 16 rectangular pieces. With the melons ball scoop out 16 balls

Filling
 In the medium bowl mix well the following ingredients

16 tofu balls, crushed
8 0z of fresh crabmeat
 4 oz of ground pork (or minced shrimp)
1/2t each salt and pepper
1t sugar
1egg
2T oyster sauce
A dash of hot oil and sesame oil
Cornstarch for dusting

 Dust 16 pieces of tofu lightly with cornstarch; fill them up equally with filling, smooth out the top. This step can be done a day ahead.
 In a large nonstick skillet, with medium high heat and enough oil to make a thick coat to the bottom of pan, cook both sides of the tofu until golden. Delicious with peanut sauce, plum sauce or just the way it is!

*May be brushed with scallion oil, or vegetable oil and bake in the oven of 350-degree for 45 minutes.

Quick plum sauce
2/3 cup of plum jam
2T rice vinegar
1/2t salt
2T coarsely chopped crystal ginger
1T hot pepper flake

With low heat and small sauce pan, melt jam adding the rest ingredients, turn heat off and let it cool until ready to use.

Lady under the Rainbow
1 block of firm tofu, slice into 8 pieces, cross wise.
1/4t each salt, pepper and hot pepper flakes
Cornstarch for dusting

Vegetables
One of each bell pepper; yellow, red, orange small julienne cut
2oz bean thread, soaked in warm water for 15 minutes then blanch in boiling water for 15 seconds, rinsed.
2T black sesame seed, toasted.

Dressing
In a medium bowl mix well

1Tcrushed garlic
1Tcrushed ginger
3T light soy sauce
3T Mirin wine- option-
3T rice vinegar
2T sugar
1T garlic oil
1T scallion oil
2t sesame oil

Mix slices tofu with salt, pepper and hot pepper (if use) dust with cornstarch. Set aside.
Into a non-stick skillet with medium high heat and light coat of oil, brown tofu on both sides, let tofu cool off then stack it up and cut them into slices.

In a large bowl, put tofu, cut up peppers, bean thread, toss well with dressing, mound salad into a large plate, sprinkle black sesame over top.

Garnish with a combination of cilantro and fresh mint.

Serves 4 as appetizer 2 as main course

Note: How can you tell when the black sesame is toasted? It's hard to detect, but you can use the aroma as a guide. With medium heat and non-stick skillet, stir constantly for 1 to 2 minutes. Have a chilled baking sheet nearby, immediately move the toasted sesame from skillet into the chilled baking sheet to stop the cooking process.

If you live in Maine, you can always use the snow bank by your door for that purpose.

Paula's Bad Week

She has been a gem for years. She starting coming to see me in my early days at Buck Street, then she followed me to Orono. The feeling is mutual because I adore her to say the least. We usually take time to visit and that brightens my day.

One day, she showed up and looked totally distressed. She tossed her shopping bag on top of the hot tar and said "I had the worst week last week". Immediately I thought of all the bad stuff one human being could possibly endure but wasn't at all prepared for her answer.

"Remember the container of tofu I bought last week? Well, I had to go to *Linens n' Things* for fifteen minutes and when I go back to my car Peaches ate the whole thing. I had to go through a week without tofu!" I was speechless.

Peaches is Paula's cute little dog.

Sophisticated Lady

This dish has it all; taste, looks, and health benefits. I just can't ask for more in one dish.

Best of all, it's really quick to prepare and keeps very well as a leftovers.

2 blocks of firm tofu cut into cubes
1t each salt and pepper
Cornstarch for dusting

In a med bowl or plastic bag mixed the above, set aside.

Paste
1T garlic oil, 1T scallion oil and hot oil to your desire
2T grated ginger
2T crushed garlic
1 to 2T turmeric

In a small bowl mix the above, set aside

Vegetables and sauce
1 pint of sweet grape tomatoes blanched in boiling water, peeled.
2 cups cooked dark red kidney beans
1/2 cup black olives (Option)
1 cup of broth
4 to 6 heads of baby Bok Choy or 8oz fresh spinach

In a large nonstick skillet with high heat sauté the paste until fragrant, lightly brown tofu, add grape tomatoes, beans and black olives (if use). Spend a little time here before adding the broth, and bring it to boil, cover and simmer for 10 minutes. At half time add your green, adjust taste, a bit more salt if needed, a bit sugar might be used it all depends on the performance of the tomatoes you use.

Lady in Good Company
Here is a vegetables patty to serve with a bun or just the way it is.

1lb of firm tofu, drained, dry off and crumble it into a large bowl
1 small sweet onion minced
1cup chopped celery, squeezed out water
2T soy sauce mixed with 1T corn starch
1 vegetable bouillon cube (prefer no salt added) crushed
1/4 cup chopped scallion.
2T chopped cilantro or herb of your choice
Black pepper

1/2 cup Panko breadcrumbs in a large non-stick skillet with a thin layer of oil sauté onion until lightly brown, add celery and cook about 2 to 3 minutes, pour in soy sauce and bouillon. Remove from heat, pour cooked vegetables into tofu, mix well, and add herb and scallion. Chill, until cold to the touch or overnight.

Divide mixture into 6 patties gently dip both sides to coat with Panko and cook it in a large non-stick skillet with just a thin layer of oil until golden brown. Serve at once.

The Gnome from Belfast
The midday sun was bright and warm over the Belfast market. I was a new member that year. Very quickly, I made new friends and for the most part, I thought I was well liked until *she* came along. She's about five feet tall and at first sight I immediately thought of the ceramic gnomes from my friend

Emma's garden. Since she was so short when she hunched over, her long nose pointed right over the food, lines of deep wrinkles etched her face. "What is this?" She points at the tofu dish.

"Its tofu, ma'am" I replied politely.

"I don't like tofu!" She said bluntly.

"Well, it's tofu, so either you love it or hate it, because there is no middle ground when it comes to this type of food."

"I looked it up in the internet and found out tofu is very bad for you, it makes you age," Her voice almost hissing as she turned her back and started to limp away.

Good Lord, I thought to myself. I didn't want to deal with this so I kept my cool, stayed calm, and rustled up a smile for the customers who were standing in line.

"Gee, what do I know, considering I've eaten tofu my entire life and here I am almost sixty years old."

She pivoted her little head around the way Linda Blair did in the Exorcist movie, nothing spared me from the words that flew out of her mouth.

"You are a liar!" she shouted. Her screeching voice caused people to turn their heads toward us. I felt sort of uneasy and embarrassed for her.

How does anyone respond to such scene? I didn't know what to say. Luckily I spotted my purse nearby, quickly grab it, pulled out my driver's license and showed it to her. At the same time I wondered to myself "why do I have to prove anything to this stranger?"

"I won't believe a word that comes out of your mouth" With those last words she scurried away from my table leaving behind a lot of stunned faces, mine included. One of the young men standing in line chuckles "Good Lord. I bet I know why she was so angry, the gnome is probably not even sixty."

See, I'm not the only one who thought so.

Stuffy Lady

Meaty Portabella mushrooms stuffed with creamy and soft tofu along side with scallions, ginger and a touch of wine. Is it elegant or delicious? Surprisingly, both!

1lb of medium firm tofu drained and crushed.
2t corn starch
2 stalks of scallion, minced
2t ginger minced
3/4t each salt and pepper
1 large egg
4 large or 6 medium Portabella caps
2t rice wine

Sauce
In a small bowl mix well, set aside.
1/4 cup light soy sauce
1T rice vinegar
2t sugar or honey
2t sesame oil
Dust mushroom lightly with cornstarch.

In a medium mixing bowl, combine crushed tofu, scallion, ginger, salt, pepper egg and wine, mix well and divide evenly over mushroom caps.

Unless you have a very large skillet, you might need to do it in two batches. In a heavy skillet with a thin layer of oil using medium high heat, brown the cap side first; for about a minute, gently flip it over and brown the tofu side, this step will take about 4 to 5 minutes. Drizzle a bit more oil as needed. Cover pan, cook an additional 3 minutes and turn off heat.

Drizzle sauce over mushrooms and serve with rice.

Rice and Noodles

I'm pretty sure you don't want to hear how much I like rice, so, I will not repeat that. I just want to share a little story of my life that is associated with this item.

As a kid I can remember, once a week, the rice merchant would carry rice to our door for purchase. I was always there to help my mother with selection. The amount of rice we consumed depended on the budget she had for that week.

Believe me, I didn't get to eat all the rice I wanted (talking about a traumatizing childhood) because my mother would make sure we ate plenty of vegetables and tofu. So it was safe to say that's where my obsession with rice was born. Until this day, I plan my meals around it.

Once, I had a bet with my husband; if he gave up watching sports and drinking beer then I would give up my chocolate and rice for a whole week. While my opponent had no problem because he had one heck of a time watching me suffers through the long week. Since then, I've learn my lesson, I can give up chocolate or sweet treats but rice, no way!

The Numbers According to Samantha

When I was in the hospital to deliver my third child, my husband had the front seat to watch me endure over twenty hours of hard core labor. Still, after all that time the baby won't drop. I was in such agonizing pain I was begging the doctor to kill me and pull her out; instead he performed a C-section. No wonder she didn't come out. She was four ounces away from ten pounds. I couldn't push this kid out even if someone put a gun to my head.

A week later I still cannot bend over to put on my socks so my husband sweetly offered to help and I let him. When he was done he affectionately said, "Honey, you should think about cutting down on the rice because when the doctor lifted your lower abdominal to pull Samantha out, I saw a lot of fat in there." He thought that was funny.

This story should end here, but it does not. That very same child grew up and named that part of me Number One. With her father's endorsement, they make a very good team, making fun of me and my rice, naming my stomach Number One and Number Two (my upper abdominal).

"Be careful Mom, unless you want Number Two to catch up with Number One in volume" my daughter would always say when I reached for my second bowl of rice.

Both Numbers go into reserve from time to time, but by no stretch of the imagination will they ever retire. I assume I'll take them with me to my grave because I would never give up my rice. So Sam will always have a reason to make fun of me.

People often say "I would do anything for my kid." I do know what that means.

Brown Rice

I recently took up brown rice. It's good for you my husband told me, not just one time, but over and over like a broken record.

It would be a piece of cake if my mother only fed me this type of rice since the day I learned how to chew, then I wouldn't have to go through this kind of pain.

If you are a serious rice enthusiast, I'm sure you would own a rice cooker. This is the one piece of equipment that will help to make your life easier. Set it up and it's done. Not a problem if you don't have one.

2 cups of brown rice

Put rice in a medium saucepan and rinse. Pour in 3 and 1/2 cup of water and let it soak for one hour before turning on the heat, same method as you cook any other rice.

While brown rice is not as good as white rice- to me- it makes pretty decent fried rice.

Jasmine or Long Grain Rice

2 cups Jasmine or long grain rice

Put rice in a medium saucepan, fill up with water, swirl around and drain. Repeat this process three or four times. Put in around 3 cups of water and bring it to boil. It's takes between seven to nine minutes, depending on your stove's power. Stir, cover, and lower heat and simmer for about fifteen to seventeen more minutes or until water is completely absorbed. Turn heat off. Let's stand for ten more minutes before serving.

Tip: Read rice label, if it says new crop, cut down on water.

Special Day Fried Rice

It's only takes about 15 minutes to prepare, then sit back, relax and enjoy!

3 to 4 cups cooked rice, cooled
1 small sweet onion, diced

8oz shrimp, minced
4oz pork, diced small
1 Chinese sausage (option) thinly sliced
1cup frozen peas or your favorite vegetables

Sauce
1/3 cup broth
2T soy sauce
1T oyster sauce
1t sugar

In a wok with high heat swirl in 2T oil, sauté onion until light brown at the edge, add pork and sausage (if use) cook until loses its pink, put in shrimp. Stir constantly for about two minutes then adding the rice. When rice is hot to the touch, about three to four minutes slowly drizzle in the sauce. Last, adding peas, cook until peas heated through.

Vegetable Fried Rice
This rice will go with just about anything, or just the way it is!

3 to 4 cup cooked rice, cooled
1 small sweet onion, diced
1T crushed garlic
1cup cooked vegetables such as peas, corn, and carrots diced

Sauce
1/4 cup broth
2T soy sauce
3/4t sugar
2T chopped scallion

Into the wok with high heat and 2T oil sauté onion until light brown at the edge add garlic, stir around for about 20 seconds, put in rice, when rice hot to the touch, add vegetables then slowly pour in sauce. Stir constantly for a few minutes; remove from heat toss in scallions, black pepper if desired.

Red rice
Spicy and exotic! Pile it up next to some roasted pork.

4 cups cooked rice, cooled
1/4 cup shallot, minced
2 cloves of garlic, crushed

1 red jalapeno pepper, minced (option)
1T creamy peanut butter
1cup red bell pepper, diced

Sauce
1/4 cup broth
1T of fish sauce
1T soy sauce
2T ketchup
*1T Sriracha chili sauce or your favorite hot sauce
1/4 cup chopped cilantro for garnish (option)

In a large non-stick skillet or wok, with high heat and 2 to 3T of oil sauté shallot until fragrant, add garlic and watch it like a hawk, toss in hot pepper if use and peanut butter, wait a minute here before adding bell pepper. When the pepper hot to the touch, toss in the rice. This is the point where you can make it good or great. Hold wok firmly with one hand, stir vigorously with other, drizzle in a bit more oil if needed. The rice kernel should be tender but crisp at the edge, that's the time to slowly pour in the sauce, cook until sauce is totally absorb, remove from heat add cilantro -only if you want it-
*The Korean hot peppers paste can be use here for a change of taste.

Green Rice
As early as May you can find spinach at your local Farmer's market. It's a reward after a long dragged on Maine winter.

2T vegetable oil or olive oil
4 bulbs shallot or small onion chopped
1/2 lb fresh spinach washed, chopped
4oz mushroom, chopped
1 and 1/4 cup of long grain rice, rinse.
2 1/2cup broth
2T soy sauce
1/2t salt, 1/2t pepper (option)

In a medium sauce pan with high heat, sauté shallot until lightly brown at the edge then add mushroom and spinach, pour in broth and bring it to boil. Add rice, when it boiling again, cover and lower heat. Cook until moisture is all absorbed, turn heat off. Rest, five to ten minutes before serving. This rice goes well with any roasted meat, or just by itself.

Green Rice with a Kick
The kick is in the charred vegetables.

Paste
1 medium sweet onion just cut it in halves keeping the skin intact.
1 medium garlic bulb, unpeel.
1 large fresh Chile, hot or mild to suit your taste
1 fresh bell pepper

Over a blazing flame, char the vegetables described above until blackened on all sides. Put it in a medium bowl, cover and let it cool off. When vegetables are comfortable to touch, clean out all the blemishes and skin then put into a food processor and run it into a smooth paste. Set paste aside.

1cup long grain rice
3T olive oil
2cups vegetables or chicken stock
Salt to taste

In medium sauce pan sauté rice in oil, take a few minutes here before adding paste and stock. Bring it all to a rolling boil, lower heat, adjust flavor with salt. Cook until rice absorbs all liquid, about 25 minutes. Turn off heat and lets it rest 10 minutes before serving. Garnish with cilantro, only if you like this friendly herb, otherwise don't bother.

A good side dish to your Enchilada.

Rice for a Thought
According to Vietnamese's folk lore; People who waste rice in their lifetime are punished in hell by having to consume maggots equal to the amount of rice they wasted.

Now you know why I would not dare to waste my rice.

An Afternoon with the Ladies
The year was 1976: I was a young bartender in Long Beach, California.

Navy customers would come and go. I had seen them all, young and old. Nice and not so nice, it didn't matter. I had one rule and sometimes that rule made me unpopular- I did not date customers. Although, there was one time because, after all, rules were meant to be broken.

I had seen him before, young, and no doubt he was a Navy boy just passing through. He'll make his move soon, I just know, I thought to myself. I have that nauseated sixth sense. After a small usual chitchat, he came right to the point.

"What are you going to do this weekend? Do you have time to show me where the best food in town is?" He smiled, flashing his even white teeth.

"Well, let's see! I brought a stereo last month, I think it's time for me to bite the bullet and try to set it up, I'm sure it'll be a piece of cake. NOT!" I said.

"I can do it for you, free of charge."

"Sure you do" I said it to myself, and then the light bulb flashed in my head. I smiled,

"As matter of fact, if you don't mind hanging out with me and my three gal friends, this Sunday lunch is my turn to host, the food will be my payment for your help. What do you think?

"I'll be in heaven!" He jumped right in.

He was not. No man in their right mind would want to be in the same room with four women who are eating and talking. We were all talking at the same time because not even one of us was fond of listening. That wasn't the worst part: the fact that we were speaking Vietnamese must have sounded like we put him in the middle of a chicken barn at feeding time (my husband says that about any group of ladies). I have no doubt about that. But he was sweet and with good nature he opened all the packages and got right to work. Then the magic words everybody was waiting for, "Let's eat!" I happily announced when all my chores were finished.

The look in his face when I set this platter of noodles in front of him was worth more than a thousand pictures. Ask anyone if they knew what Pad Thai was over thirty years ago just see if you can get an answer. The young man's eyes popped out at the sight of red shrimp curled up against the pearly white rice noodles. Green herbs cascaded from top to bottom with bean sprouts, fresh roasted peanuts, and a small bowl of peanut sauce with coconut cream accompanied with everybody's plate. Of course, I had to take punches from the women (they accusing me of showing off).

He set up the stereo system, showed me how to use it and thanked me sincerely for his lunch. We teased him with advice, "You should marry a Thai girl, be a good husband to her, and the supply of a lifetime of rice noodle is yours to keep".

About a year later we got a postcard from our young Navy friend. He didn't take our counsel because he was getting married to a Vietnamese girl named Linda, half Vietnamese, and half American.

That might work!

Sunday Noodles and Shrimp with Coconut
1lb of dried rice noodles
12oz of fresh bean sprouts
A large sweet onion, sliced thin

A bundle of cilantro, chopped.
A bunch of scallions, chopped.
A cup of fresh roasted peanuts, coarsely chopped
1lb of large shrimp, cleaned, deveined, butterfly cut

Marinade for shrimp
1/4t each salt and black pepper
1t garlic powder
1T of cornstarch
1t of garlic oil or vegetable oil

Sauce
In a small bowl mixed well:
1/2 cup of broth
1T oyster sauce
1T fish sauce
1T soy sauce
1T white vinegar
2t sugar

In a medium bowl marinate shrimp, set aside.
Cook rice noodle until tender but firm. Drain run cold water through it, set aside.
With highest temperature, heat wok up to a smoking point, drizzle in 3 T vegetable oil, than put in shrimp. It's important to scatter shrimp around, to create a little burn at the edge for taste. When shrimp curls up and turns color add onion, scallion and stir fry for about two minutes, add bean sprouts, stir well and pour in sauce.
Making sure shrimp is cooked through before setting in the noodles. Turn noodles around so they become well coated with sauce, and are evenly heated.
Pour in a large serving plate, scatter cilantro and peanuts over the top; serve with coconut sauce. This dish will do well all by itself, but the bonus sauce makes it smooth and sensual to your taste buds.

Coconut and lime sauce
1/2 cup boiling broth
1/3 cup smooth peanut butter
1/3 cup coconut cream or 3 T dried coconut powder
1/4 cup sugar
2, 3 T of fish sauce or soy sauce
2, 3 T of fresh squeezed lime juice

Freshly chopped Jalapeno pepper to your taste
2 cloves of garlic crushed

Mix all ingredients together, proceed careful with fish sauce and lime juice.

My Twin Kay: the Bonus

Okay, so we aren't joined by the term "twin" by birth but so what? We still can be twins
for whatever reason we think is important.

Number one we shared an enormous passion for good chocolate and a lot of it, the cheap stuff just doesn't count. We both agree on this issue wholeheartedly.

Number two, we are picky about food.

And number three, which is the most important, we as a team are fond of complaining.

The way we figure it God created women for this particular task and we must craft it to perfection and carry on the torch. Who are we to go against God's will? That's why the mission must go on and this is where we take turns to be good or evil. I can't speak for Kay's husband but I know whenever I practice the art of complaining in any form, my husband stares me down as if I was possessed by the devil. Judging by his reactions he must think I have been evil all my life, but that's not true. Kay can testify to this on my behalf; I told her the whole story how I was a sweet and totally nice individual, before my dear husband worked his magic and transformed me into a nagging wife (only a quarter of truth).

I met her almost twenty years ago on a job I catered for a group of business women; she was one of them. What's funny is that even if someone beat me over the head with a wooden stick I still can't come up with any other name from that job.

Kay has the ability to make me laugh and I do know how to amuse her, she loves gardening and she loves food! We're really identical twins over these two subjects.

One afternoon, some years ago, she was weeding. I leaned over her fence and told her I was going to write a cook book and that she'd be the one to help me (it was really that easy).

So for the next many Tuesdays, I would have lunch on the table ready when she arrived and we would devour the food, complain about everything from the annoying household chores, to the bad weather, and the very best subject: "our loving mates". When we were done with lunch, I would hand her my hand written notes, stories, and recipes and she would be the one to type them and put it into the text.

I'll spare Kay this time because since then I've learned how to use the computer (sort of).

Until this day, Kay remains the best bonus I got from that job.

Kay's Rice Noodles

One of Kay favorite dishes is the grilled pork with rice noodle from my first book but I know she will never want to put up with that much of work, so I designed this dish to simplify the process and still obtained the taste that will satisfy even Kay's picky taste buds.

Meat and vegetables

1 small pork tenderloin; about 1lb
1/2t each salt, pepper
1T finely chopped lemongrass
2T garlic oil or vegetable oil
1 package of rice noodles 14-16oz
1package of bean sprouts 12oz, rinsed
1/4 cup of each cilantro, mint and crispy shallot

Sauce

3T fish sauce
3T water
3T sugar
2T lime juice or vinegar
2T each mince garlic and hot chili such as Serrano or jalapeno

In a small bowl mix sauce, set aside.

Place tenderloin lengthwise on a large cutting board, with a sharp knife make the first cut about 1/2 inch in from the right edge, don't cut it all the way through, leave about 1/2 inch from the bottom, with your left hand roll the thick side of pork as you cut towards the left, keep cutting in this way until you end up with a piece of pork that is flat and near 1/2 inch thick. Rub pork evenly with salt, peppers and lemongrass, last, but not least brush with oil, then set it aside.

Cook rice noodles according to the package, about five minutes, rinse, drain, and set it over a large serving plate

In a medium skillet with a thin layer of oil and high heat, sear pork until brown and cook through, about 8-10 minutes. Remove meat, put in bean sprouts stir around just until warm but not cooked. Transfer bean sprouts over noodles. When meat is cool enough to handle; slice it, and place meat on top of bean sprouts. Top it all with herbs, crispy shallots and serve with sauce.

Baby Love's Rice Noodles with Tofu and Bean Sprouts

Samantha is our youngest daughter. She has many nicknames given to her by different members of our family. Baby love is the one I have given her.

In the last book, I described Sam's eating habits- everything and anything fried. That same child is growing and so are her eating habits. Recently she came home for the holiday and requested rice noodles with tofu.

Evidently she has been putting a lot of tofu into her daily meals. I can't say that I'm surprised, as parents we have learned one thing: if you keep on preaching, something will get through sooner or later. This time the mighty tofu has spoken. Wow! She asks for tofu instead of steak and French fries, sorry Dad. This is indeed a historic event!

I jumped right in and designed this particular dish for her. It's takes a bit of work but I am pleased with the result. I'll walk you through this production, step by step, but the play is all yours to conduct. If you don't want tofu, substitute this item for whatever protein of your choice. However, a good tasting vegetarian dish is always a prize winner in my book.

Tofu
1 block of extra firm tofu, drained, dry with paper towel
1t salt
1t sugar
3/4 t each onion and garlic powder
1T corn starch

Cut tofu into a medium julienne sticks, place it in to a large bowl, and gently toss with the spices above. Let it rest, this step can be done ahead,

1lb of rice noodles soaked in water for 30 minutes, drain.

Vegetables
1 package of bean sprouts 12oz
1lb of Napa cabbage, shredded into small julienne cut to match the noodles
1 medium sweet onion, slices thin
1T crushed garlic

Sauce
3/4 cup of broth
2T light soy sauce
*2T fish sauce
**1-2T sugar
***1-2T tamarind extract
A handful of cilantro- or Thai basil- chopped.

A handful of crispy shallot
Coarsely chopped roasted peanut-option-

Blanch the soaked and well drained noodles in boiling water for 2 minutes, drain, rinse with cold water, and let them drain again.

*Mix the sauce, if you want to do it the vegan way, omit the fish sauce and increase the soy sauce.

** proceed with 1T sugar first, you can always add a bit more as the show goes on.

*** Depending on where the tamarind extracted comes from, the homemade one is less tart than the one in a concentrated bottle, if you don't have it handy, substitute with white vinegar.

Do the checklist before turning on the heat, the prepped tofu, vegetables, noodles, sauce, and garnish. It's show time!

In a large nonstick skillet with a thin layer of oil and high heat, sauté the onion until slightly brown at the edge, adding garlic, watching it like a hawk at this point, you don't want the garlic to burn, at the same time, the garlic won't be able to deliver its good unless it has a chance to work with the oil and the heat.

The noodles are next on the list; stir them constantly, but, gently. When the noodles are a bit brown at the edge, swirl in about 1/2 cup of sauce- reserve the rest for the next step- toss gently until all the noodles absorb their fair share and are hot to the touch.

Transfer noodles into a large and deep serving platter, set aside.

Clean out the skillet, with a thin coat of oil, lightly brown tofu, top it all off with bean sprouts and Napa cabbages. Gently fold the vegetables into tofu, drizzle in the rest of sauce. Taste, transform it into your own. Toss in the herb and pour everything over noodles with crispy shallot and chopped peanut.

The tender noodles should be laced with the velvety soft and creamy tofu, lightly sweet with a bit of tangy overtone. Nutty peanuts combined with cilantro and crisp shallots. This is the trademark belonging to Thai and Vietnamese cuisine.

The Special of Everyday Vegetables

The Leaf is Beautiful!

The summer of 2009 we joined the Castine market. My husband and Samantha tended to it while I was at the usual place in Northeast Harbor. When Northeast ended the last week in August, I went to Castine for the rest of the season. By then, even if it was still open, the numbers of customers were falling next to nothing. But I made my bed so I had no other choice but to lay in it.

The last two weeks before it ended for the season, it was so bad you could actually count the number of customers on one hand. I'll be the first one to admit that I have no patience if I set out to do something new, including a new market or a new dish. It better show me a good result real quick or it's out of the door and I'll be gone.

So here I am, with the table almost full of food plus extra items people requested. I didn't see any of them show up. I was agitated to say the least, and it was building up as it got nearer to closing time. They were still not there. I was getting angry!

The woman next to my table was trying to make small talk with me, which I was avoiding because, number one, I didn't know her and, number two, I was in a bad mood and she was far too cheerful (even if she didn't sell much of anything either). Right there, that attitude already makes her a better person than I am. So, in one hand she kept on talking and on the other hand I was holding up my expressionless face and trying not to respond at all. The pressure cooker inside me was building up, and up, and then, finally, it exploded when I heard her latest happy chirp, "Well, at least we have some beautiful leaves to look at".

I tried very hard to keep the tone of my voice even but I don't think I was trying to be that good of an actress.

"I'm so glad that you are able to enjoy the scenery right now, I'm here for business and right now the business is really crappy!" I said.

If she got my drift, I don't know. It doesn't seem to bother her in anyway. I wish I could say the same for me because I was loathing my words all the way home and the rest of that day. Here was this nice lady and even on her very best day I was positive that my business made out better than hers and yet I behaved badly to say the least. I should be ashamed of myself. Yes, I am. I'll try to be a better person the next round when we see each other again. In the meantime, please except my sincere apology, I'm sorry!

Asparagus with Crab Meat and Ground Pork
I grew up with this dish, one of the many specialty dishes I learned from my mother

1lb of fresh asparagus, trimmed, cut about 2 inches long

Soak asparagus in cold water for 1/2 an hour before cooking time, this process delivers a firmer bite. Drain, and blanch in boiling water for 1 minute.

Pork
8oz of lean ground pork
1/2t each salt, pepper and sugar
2t cornstarch

In a small bowl, mix the above ingredients, set aside.

Crab and sauce
2T vegetable oil for stir fry
8oz fresh crab meat
1/2 cup seafood stock, clam juice or chicken broth
2T light soy sauce
2t sesame oil

In wok with high heat, when a wisp of smoke appear drizzle in oil, sauté pork until there is no more pink and it is lightly browned at the edge then add asparagus and stir fry for one minute.
Pour in stock and bring it to boil for another minute before allowing the crab to make its entrance. When it almost boils again, add sesame oil, remove from heat and serve it immediately. A mound of rice by its side would make a good companion.

Broccoli
I come from Vietnam so there was no such thing as broccoli when I was growing up.
From the first day I got here I have been thankful for this great country and for the gift of broccoli.

Unless you have a garden of your own, the farmers market is your best bet for this item. Fresh picked broccoli is sweet, firm, crunchy, and yet, it's tender to your bite. Avoid any limp broccoli with large buds. Pick broccoli with a deep dark color. Not only will they taste better but they are the ones packed with more nutritional value.

The florets are rich in vitamins but I believed the stalks have more fiber power. Believe me, I can do so much with this fantastic vegetable, but my favorite way is to steam it up for four to five minutes and drizzle with a mixture of soy sauce, lemon juice and a touch of toasted sesame seeds.

Bok Choy

This is one the most popular vegetables in China, ask any Chinese to see if they don't agree. From a gardener's point of view, this vegetable needs to be used as soon as it is cut because it tends to lose its sweetness. I recommend the baby type, no larger than the palm of your hand. Wash it thoroughly under each leaf. Bring water to a rolling boil and blanch for one minute. From there, it is ready for action in stir fry or for just dipping it into soy vinegar dressing for a delicious low calorie treat.

A Wild Green meets Beef

You can do this dish in a flash if you have the fiddleheads all clean and ready to cook.

A pint of fiddleheads, blanched in boiling water for 5-6 minutes until tender but firm, chill. This step can be done a day ahead.
1lb of flank steak, sliced thin across the grain mixed with 1T garlic oil, set aside

Sauce
2T soy sauce
1t of sugar
Have it ready
2T gin
2T-crushed garlic
Freshly ground black pepper

The process I'm using in this dish is called "dry fry" quick to make, and quick to serve.

Heat wok with high heat, swirl lightly with oil. Stir-fry garlic and beef, work fast and move quickly. Do not allow beef to turn runny.

Next step is to flash in gin, at this point beef should be a bit brown at the edge, and then you might add the greens, when they are hot to the touch, stir in sauce, toss well. Remove from heat serve at once.

Napa Cabbage

This is the cabbage of choice for me to stir fry, add to rice or noodle dishes. Flavor always comes first but time saving is another reason. If time is tight, it can be cooked in less than three minutes, whether it's for soup or sauté.

Try this recipe. It takes take a few minutes to prepare, store it in an air tight container and it will last at least a month in the refrigerator. Great for a snack, totally makes a good sidekick to any sandwich, but is also not a bad choice to team up with a piece of roasted pork or chicken.

Cabbage

1 small head of Napa cabbage, quarter lengthwise then cut crosswise to 2inch
1 small daikon, sliced thin then cut to 2-3inch
1bunch of green onion cut same length as cabbages
3T salt

In a large mixing bowl, toss well so all the vegetables get a chance to coat with salt. Cover, refrigerator overnight.

Dressing

2T ginger, crushed
1 garlic bulb peeled and crushed.
2T white vinegar
*1T sugar

Korean hot pepper flakes, this is a very important ingredient, so, you can use from 2T to 1/4 cup, the Korean peppers are spicy but they're not very hot (to my taste) sometimes I even add cayenne on top of it all.

Drain cabbage, squeeze out excess water and mix until it well blended with dressing. Store as described.

*Use a little bit more sugar if you have a sweet tooth like I do.

String Beans

Simple and delicious!
1lb of fresh string beans washed and trimmed.
2T vegetable oil
2T minced fresh garlic
1T each oyster sauce and soy sauce
Coarse salt and freshly ground pepper to your taste

In a large pan with boiling water, blanch beans for exactly 5 minutes; don't time it right after putting beans into boiling water, start to time when the water boils again, 6 minutes for larger beans.

While beans are in the hot pot, (about two minutes left from the cooking time described) sauté garlic in a large skillet with medium heat, watch it like a hawk and don't let it burn. Drain beans and add it immediately to the aromatic garlic, spend about 1 minute here and keep the stirring motion alive, drizzle in soy and oyster sauce, sprinkle in the salt and pepper at this point and turn heat off.

This simple string bean makes a special side dish with any roasted meat.

Tossed String Bean with Sesame Ginger

This is another favorite dish of beans I often prepare at home, especially in the summer. Leftovers never seem to interfere with the quality of this dish.

2lbs of young and fresh beans

Cook in boiling water for four to five minutes drain and transfer cooked beans into a large, deep serving plate.

Dressing
1T fresh grated ginger
1T rice vinegar or white vinegar
2T light soy sauce
1T garlic oil
1t sugar
1t toasted sesame oil
1/2t each salt and freshly ground black peppers.
2T freshly toasted sesame seed

Pour dressing over beans; toss until they are well blended with dressing. A touch of hot oil maybe added for a kick.

Corn with Coconut Cream

This is my own version of Corn Maque Choux. For me, time in the summer is always tight but I always try to make this dish at least once, before fresh out of the garden sweet corn is just a memory.

4cups of fresh corn kennels- about ½ dozen- Silver Queen corn- if you can find it.
1/2 cup chopped sweet onion
1/2 cup chopped red bell peppers
Salt and peppers to taste
1/2 cup coconut cream
Green onion, cilantro, minced fresh hot peppers such as Thai dragon or Serrano

In a large skillet with medium high heat, sauté onion until lightly brown, then add peppers and cook just until you can detect the aroma, put in corn and coconut cream, bring it all to boil for two minutes, adjust taste with salt.

Remove from heat, toss in fresh herbs and hot peppers-if use- Serve at once.

Wheat free Tempura Vegetables
1/2 cup corn starch
1/4 cup potato starch
1/2t baking powder
3/4t each salt, pepper
1t sesame oil
*Water from 3/4 cup to 1 cup
Vegetables can be asparagus, string beans, egg plant, portabella mushroom etc...

Whatever choice of veggies in use; make sure they are dried well before dipping them in batter, keep oil's temperature steady around 350 degree. Don't crowd pan.

If a bit of batter is left; just throw in some slices of sweet onion to use it up. What can I say? I came from a third world country; I don't feel comfortable to throw anything away.

*Use iced cold water for a crispier coat.

Swiss chard
It's a rare occasion when I eat cheese with a vegetables but I like it in this simple dish.

2 bunches of rainbow chard, wash each stem to clear off grit
1T butter
2T olive oil
1 bulb of garlic clove, clean and crushed
2T light soy sauce
2T fresh grated Parmesan cheese
2T fresh grated Asiago cheese
Juice of half lemon and freshly cracked black pepper

In a large soup pan with water at a rolling boil, blanch chard to your desired tenderness, drain. Plunge it into cold water and squeeze out excess moisture, cut to bite size length.

This step can be done a day ahead.

In a large skillet, heat butter and olive oil until hot but not smoking; sauté garlic until aromatic but not brown, stir in soy sauce before tossing in the vegetables; cook just enough to heat it up. Turn heat off, mix well with cheese, lemon juice and black peppers.

Serve at once.

Cauliflower

I like the chore of raising cauliflower. I enjoy and admire the tiny head as it forms until the day it has matured into a large beautiful big head. Sadly I have to put it to use so there is no more candy for my eyes.

It's easy to spot fresh cauliflower with its green young leaves and the white head (the colored varieties are for the birds).I like my cauliflower old-fashioned.

I've seen vendors at the farmer markets strip away most of the green outer leaves, that should not happen. These young leaves really are succulent and tender. Here is my quickest version of how I like to prepare the queen. By the way, broccoli is the king in my book, but cauliflower is the queen.

1 head of cauliflower, with young, green outer leaves intact
2T vegetable oil
1T crushed fresh ginger
1/2 cup broth
2T soy sauce
Salt and pepper to taste
Herb of your choice, mine would be chopped green scallion in this dish.

Cut vegetable white and green into bite size, wash and let it drain

In a wok with high heat, swirl in oil stir, fry the ginger for about 30 seconds, immediately toss in cauliflower, stir it around about 2 to 3 minutes, pour in broth and soy sauce, toss well and cover it up with lid.

Three to four minutes for tender crisp. Five to six minutes for tender soft.

Pepper and green herb will be the last to add. Remove from heat

As with any other vegetable serve as soon as you can for best flavor and texture.

Eggplant

Once upon a time, when my children were young, we had a big garden and I would forever try to grow eggplant. We love eggplant, my husband and I, but the kids hated it with a passion. They wouldn't even eat it as eggplant parmesan. One would think that anything drenched in cheese and tomatoes would change their minds but not with my kids.

One lucky year Mother Nature was kind enough to shower us with lots of rain and sunshine and we had so many eggplants. The children suggested we should set up a table next to the road to sell and get rid of this vile vegetable.

Let me tell you! The Americans of years ago were totally different than the Americans of today or maybe it was just in this small town of Winterport that was close minded because nobody wanted eggplant. They didn't even know what it was! All day, the question repeated itself, "What is this?"

"It's eggplant"

"How do you cook it?"

"You can grill it, put it in curry of all kinds, my quick way is stir fry it"

"Sorry! We only eat meat and potatoes"

Needless to say we didn't make a sale. My freezer was filled up with curry and eggplant ratatouille that year.

This is a quick and delicious way to enjoy this vegetable.
2lbs of slim egg plant
A hand full of dried shiitake mushrooms, soaked in warm water for at least 30 minutes
1/4 cup Mirin
1/4 cup broth from soaking shiitake mushroom
1/4 cup soy sauce
2t sugar
2t sesame oil

Wash egg plant, trim away both ends, hold it firmly with your left hand, make the first cut diagonally into approximately ¾ of an inch slice, rotate egg plant to an angle then cut again, this will result in round edged triangle chunky nuggets, set aside. Remove mushrooms from soaking liquid, squeeze out excess moisture and slice them into thin slices In a wok with high heat and a thin swirl of oil, sauté egg plant for about one minute, add slices of mushroom, spend another minute here before adding wine, broth and sugar. Cover, let it cook for about 2 to 3 minutes, open up slowly drizzle in soy sauce and taste as you proceed further. Remove from heat and sprinkle in sesame oil.

Serve soon as you can for best flavor.

*Note: I don't use any ginger, garlic or onion for a reason; by crossing them out, the wine will work its magic with shiitake mushroom. You'll taste it, bold and musky!

Potato Patties

Don't think for a minute that I'm making hash browns here. These addictive little morsels will beg you to keep popping them into your mouth. Form it as a big patty for a side dish, or a smaller version as an appetizer

Leading role
3 to 4 medium sized Yukon gold potatoes*, peeled shredded, mixed with 2t salt, place it in a colander and let it drip over the sink about 15 minutes.

Squeezed away all excess moisture and place it in a medium bowl.

Supporting cast
1 small sweet onion, thinly sliced
1/3 cup cornstarch
1 egg
1T curry powder
1/4 cup chopped green onion
1t salt
Black peppers as desired

Show time
Back to the bowl with shredded potatoes; mix in corn starch and the rest of the cast.

In a large skillet with 1cup of vegetable oil, heat oil until hot 350 degree-not smoking- drop in mixture by tablespoon full for appetizer, flatten it with a wooden spoon and fry until golden of both sides.

If you want to steer clear of good old potatoes, you might want to try it with sweet potatoes. Whatever kind of spud you use just serve it soon as possible to enjoy the flavor at its best.

*My favorite choice of potatoes is Yukon gold.

The medium size spud with a creamy, buttery texture is an excellent candidate for mashed potatoes; they don't fall apart when sliced and baked au gratin. It superbly holds its shape in soup or salad. I haven't come across all its quality in other potatoes. I don't know, maybe I really never give other potatoes a chance.

The Many Faces of Kale
This is prince among dark and leafy greens. This hardy vegetable belongs to the cabbage family. I can open a seed catalog and go crazy over the new varieties of kale that are available these days. Every year I try a different kind and I haven't run into one I dislike.

The curly type is the most common one. The Tuscan kind, also called black kale, is easiest to handle and quickest to cook. There is a red kind with curly and frilly leaves that carries a pretty mauve color in the vein. I also like the broad leaf Thai variety that has a cute white blossom. Bottom line, I like them all!

Kale holds a bold, rich taste with a pleasant chewy texture. This indicates that kale is loaded with fiber, it is an excellent source of vitamins A, C and K and calcium as well, it's no wonder I team up this green with tofu. My customers eat it right up.

You just can't go wrong when purchasing kale at your local farmers market. If you have to go to the regular grocery store for this task; make sure to pick the ones that are moist with dark green leaves.

Take time and wash it with several changes of water before using, and last but not least, blanch it first before cooking it into any dish for the best flavor and texture.

If you don't have a lot of time to squander in the kitchen I'll share with you my technique for this green, sort of a one shot with many meals to follow. Put several bundles of kale, washed and blanched in boiling water for 2-3 minutes. Drain, squeeze out excess water. Start with meal number one, sauté it with garlic and flash of soy sauce, there, it's ready for omelet, or team it up with sundried tomatoes in a frittata.

Meal number two, sauté with ginger, sprinkle in some rice wine or sherry, and scatter over some sea salt then finish it off with a touch of sesame oil. Now, you are in the Chinese cooking territory.

Meal number three, sauté with fresh garlic and chopped hot Chile, seasoning it with a touch of sugar and fish sauce. At this point, you are effortlessly conquering Thai and Vietnamese cooking.

Meal number four, sauté with bonito flake and ginger, drizzle in a touch of Mirin sweet wine, soy sauce. This is a Japanese way of using kale.

Getting sick of stir fry? You can try kale in salad, for every two bunches of blanched kale   use 1/2 cup of cranberries* 1/4 cup toasted pine nut and toss in this dressing:

1T rice vinegar
1T balsamic vinegar
1T honey
2T garlic or olive oil
1t dried hot peppers
Salt to taste

I don't know what kind of cooking this one is, it just taste good, that's all!
*Soak it for fifteen minutes for moist and tender berries.

Twenty Minutes Kidney Beans
A one dish meal, if you are up for some comfort food.

2 cans of dark red kidney beans drained, rinsed

1/2cup chopped onion
2T-crushed garlic
1T tomatoes paste
1 4oz can green chili
1 cup chopped bell pepper
1cup chopped mushroom
1cup chopped tomatoes
2 cups broth
Spices
1 to 3t quality chili powder
1T dried minced garlic
1t dried Mexican oregano
1t cumin
1t each salt and sugar
2T corn flour

In a heavy bottom Dutch pan with high heat and 2T olive oil sauté onion until lightly brown, add paste and stir-fry for a minute. This step will give the dish a beautiful color. The next step is to put in the vegetables, let it sweat out for few minutes then add broth, spices and beans. Stir well, when it come to a full boil, lower heat, cover and cook for twenty minutes. Stir occasionally. I usually team it up with rice. Grated Jack or Cheddar cheese makes a good topping.

Peppers

Sweet, or fiery hot, this is the vegetable which makes food flavor come alive!

Visit the farmers market around mid to late summer and witness the rainbow of peppers with all shapes and colors. Pick the blocky one with smooth skin and plump flesh, you just can't go wrong. Keep it dry and cold to prolong its life span.

Black Bean Patties

This item has accumulated a long list of loyal of fans over the years. But the biggest enthusiast of all must be the pint size named "King David". This loving nick name was given to him by his parents. When we first met he was no more than five years old, cute as a button, dimples in his smile, and a twinkle in his eyes. His family is from out of state and it is always a treat for me to see them in Northeast Harbor every summer.

The second biggest fan has got to be Matt, the flower man, from Bar Harbor. Everybody loves Matt because he makes it easy for everyone to love him just by being himself. He has a big heart, he has a great sense of humor and he is a generous person. That's my friend Matt. It's impossible for me to picture Bar Harbor or Northeast Harbor market without him and his breathtaking lilies.

1lb of dried black beans
2T olive oil
1 medium onion, minced.
2T garlic, crushed
1 Jalapeno pepper, minced
Spices
1t cumin
1 to 2t quality pure mild or hot chili powder
1 t each salt and pepper, more or less to your taste
1/2 cup breadcrumbs or corn starch to dust

Always sort out beans and wash them through several changes of water. This step is applied to all dried beans. A quick method is to bring them to boil, cover and let them rest for 2 hours then cook until beans tender to your desired taste.

I always soak them over night, rinse again and cover them up with water and 1/2t of baking soda- this step cuts down cooking time- Bring to boil, and then cover with lid, lower heat and simmer until beans are tender, its take 30 to 35 minutes. Drain, reserve some cooking liquid. With a pastry cutting blade, crush beans, leave bits of chunk, set aside.

In a skillet with oil sauté onion, garlic and jalapeno pepper, add this group to beans, add spices, along with 1 or 2T reserved liquid, mix well, chill until bean mixture is cold to the touch. Divide beans into 6 or 8 patties, dust with cornstarch or roll into breadcrumbs and lightly brown both sides in a large non-stick skillet with a thin layer of oil. Serve warm with salsa and sour cream if desired.

Marinated Chickpea
1lb of dried chickpeas, sorted, washed, soaked overnight.
1cup black olives, quartered
4 cloves garlic, crushed
1T ginger crushed
1t dried hot pepper flakes
2T garlic oil or olive oil
1/2t each salt and pepper
1/4 cup balsamic vinegar
1/4 cup soy sauce
Handful of mint, chopped

Rinse chick peas; put them in a large stockpot with enough water to cover, plus a few inches over. With high heat, bring it to boil before lowering the heat and let simmer until tender; about 1 hour. Drain, put chickpeas in a large bowl and toss with the rest of the ingredients. A slice of hearty bread as an accompaniment is all you need for a light meal.

For a fancier fare, mound them up on top of fresh baby spinach for extra green power.

Tip: for every pound of dried chickpeas, you'll have 6 cups of cooked.

Red Beans and Greens

This dish usually appears at my table in early October, when a bit of chill is in the air. Green chilies, red chilies, and tamarind paste add the taste of the tropics to the common beans and greens.

1 lb of dry red beans
1 lb of extra hot, good and lean sausages of your choice, cut into bite size
1 lb lean ground beef or pork
Mexican chili, mild or hot to your call, 4 to 5 chili pods
Spices
2T corn flour
2t each salt and sugar
2t good chili powder
2t cumin
2T tomatoes paste
1 cup of chopped onion
1/4 cup chopped garlic
1 to 2T concentrated tamarind paste
4 cups chopped kale, chard or your favorite greens

Place dry beans in a Dutch pan using two parts water to one part beans and bring it to boil. Cover and let it rest for 2 hours. Rinse dried chili, discard seed and break it up. Let it soak in 1 cup of boiling water (or broth) for 1/2 an hour. Puree chili pods in food processor with enough liquid to turn it into a paste. Reserve the rest of liquid, set it aside.

In a large nonstick skillet cook sausages and beef until lightly browned, add onion and garlic, spend a little time here before putting in tomato paste and spices.

Bring beans to boil again, put the prepared meat into beans together with tamarind paste, the rest of soaked chili liquid and let it simmer for an hour and a half. Stir occasionally, toss in greens, and adjust seasoning at this point, maybe a touch of your favorite hot sauce, cook until greens are tender but crisp. Top it with cheese if you wish.

Salads for All Seasons

Mayonnaise without End

I have loved mayonnaise long before I even knew what it was. Every time I got the chance to visit the neighborhood sandwich shop, the very young and chubby part of me would salivate when my eyes encountered the big fat bowl of this creamy stuff. And when they spread it over the French bread I just couldn't help but beg for extra. Then one day I asked the question I should've asked a long time before, "What is it anyway?"

"Mostly oil," The woman said

"It can't be just oil," I argued. "It's lemony yellow and it's tangy." Good lord! I was being so annoying but the woman just laughed and asked me why I wanted to know. I told her I was just curious about food. She patiently stood there and explained the whole process of how to make this tasty spread.

"You start with egg yolk, or whole egg, then slowly but steadily you drip in the oil, one drop at a time and beat it in with your other hand, until it thickens. The tangy taste comes from vinegar. It's very simple," she said.

That was my first lesson on how to make mayonnaise.

I make it with different flavors to cater to all kinds of salad. Two things to remember, whenever you make homemade mayonnaise, eat it up in two to three days max and always store it in the refrigerator.

1large egg yolk

2t of white vinegar (white wine vinegar, red wine vinegar or lemon juice)

Pinch of salt and 3/4 cup oil, canola, soy bean or olive oil.

This is the mother recipe; of course all the babies came out of her carrying all sorts of herbs, jalapeno peppers, capers, sweet pickles etc...

Thanks, the technology belongs to my food processor, which's very helpful for this task!

Cucumber

Summer is the best time to enjoy cucumbers from your local farmers market.

Most of us eat them as is (raw) but you can also put them in a stir fry or make a cold soup. My mother stir fried them with squid or shrimp. She would

118

flavor them perfectly with fish sauce, oyster sauce, and a sprinkle of green scallions for a final touch.

The cucumbers we find at the regular supermarket are usually waxed with thick skin and that's why we have to peel them. The Japanese type contains small seeds and is slender with a bumpy skin. The Persian kind is about six inches long and the Armenian kind is light with ribbed skin and usually soft. Many types at the market do not need to be peeled in order to enjoy.

Sweet and Spicy Petite Cucumber
2 - 3 lbs small cucumbers
1T salt
1/4 to 1/3 cup sugar
1/4 cup sliced fresh garlic
1/3 cup white vinegar
2 to 10 sliced jalapeno pepper

In a large bowl, mix well. Refrigerate for 24hr, now, it's ready to munch on, or use it as a side dish. Leftovers will keep well in refrigerator.

Cucumber with Herbs and Nuts
I use this dish as an appetizer. The best cucumber to use is the type with tiny seeds such as Japanese type. But really any cucumber you've got on hand will do. Slice the cucumber, make the dressing, toss in herbs and nuts, and serve it as soon as possible.

4 to 5 cups thinly sliced seedless cucumbers
1/2 cup of cup fresh roasted peanuts coarsely chopped
1/2 cup of fresh mint, torn
Dressing
1/4 cup of cup fish sauce
1/4 cup sugar
1/4 cup vinegar
2, 3T crushed garlic
1 to 5 red jalapenos minced

Sweet Potatoes in Salad
6 medium sweet potatoes
1/2 cup celery, coarsely chopped
1/4 cup sweet onion, coarsely chopped
1 to 2T curry powder
1can of coconut cream
1/4 cup vinegar

2t salt
1-2 fresh chilies like jalapeno, minced for garnish.
Heat oven to 375 degree

Place whole potatoes on a baking sheet and bake until firm to the touch. Cool.

In a large deep skillet with 2T oil, lightly sauté onion and celery with curry powder until warm. Turn heat off and pour in coconut cream. Allow it to melt while you are tending to the potatoes.

Peel the potatoes and cut to any desired size. Whisk vinegar and salt into a dressing and adjust the seasonings to please your taste buds. You may want to add a touch of sugar to displace the tartness of the vinegar. Fold the potatoes together with hot peppers into the dressing.

Serve warm or cold, scatter in some chopped green onions for a special effect

String Beans in Salad

Simply irresistible, and for the best result, grow your own beans or head straight to the farmer's market. Don't waste your time with anything less than fresh beans in this dish.

2 pounds haricots verts
4 hard boil eggs, shelled and quartered
1 medium sweet red onion sliced thin.
For the dressing
3T red wine vinegar
1/4 cup garlic oil or olive oil
2t hot oil
2T chopped shallot
2T soy sauce
1t sugar
Salt and pepper to taste

In a large Dutch pan filled 2/3 with water, bring it to rolling boil, put in beans, when all of it starts to boil again, time it for five minutes. Drain, plunge beans in iced cold water to stop the further cooking process.

In a large mixing bowl, whisk dressing until well blended together. Toss in beans and red onion, gently fold in eggs, present all this luscious in a large platter and if you are not a vegetarian, treat yourself to some crispy bacon crumbled over the top. Delicious is an understatement!

Kohlrabi in Salad

I think I know a thing or two about kohlrabi because I grew up alongside this vegetable. My mother used it in stir fry quite often. However, the task of cooking it didn't stop there. She would slow cook them with pork on a rainy day, and when we didn't have meat, she would team it up with tofu for all sorts of delightful flavors.

My very favorite version she cooked was the way she would shred it into fine sticks, toss in some salt, squeeze all the moisture out, and turn it into a lightly sweet and spicy salad.

A large bunch of young kohlrabi, about 2lbs, peel, small julienne cut
2t salt

Toss well with salt and let it rest for an hour, squeeze out excess water

Dressing
2 large garlic cloves crushed
1 or 2 chili pepper minced
3T white vinegar
2 to 3T fish sauce
3T sugar
1/4 cup shallot oil

Important supporting cast
1/2cup freshly roasted peanuts coarsely chopped
1/4 cup crispy shallots
Mint and Cilantro for herbs

Toss vegetables with dressing until well blended, transfer salad to a larger serving plate. Cascade over with all the wonderful supporting casts.

Here is the best part; leftovers are just as good as the day before.

Appleton Creamery

Caitlan is the force behind Appleton creamery. She is responsible for awards winning goat cheese and a beautiful display with wall to wall samples. Every time she can't make it to the market there are people asking for her all day. This is just the crowd's way of saying she's popular.

I owe it mostly to her for my good memories the year I was at the Belfast market. She said it was a good place to be and she was right.

There is another reason I would like to thank Caitlan. She once told me she likes my sense of humor.

"You have a good sense of humor!" She said with conviction.

Wow! This information was hitting my head like a brick. The very knowledgeable man I married over thirty years ago often reminds me that I have no sense of humor at all! Would it be an act of betrayal on my part if I take her word over his? I have only known this lady for a few years. This is certainly a predicament that I have to figure out. Anyway, because of her praise, I try my best not to disappoint my friend by going against her words. So whenever I put down anything in writing, I try my best to put a sense of hilarity on occasion. I figured that if I keep on practicing I might be good some day. When that day arrives I'll have Caitlan to be grateful for all my sense of humor.

Zucchini in Salad

What the heck you are going to do with zucchini when it seems to grow out of every plant in your garden at the peak of summer? You can only take so much of it in stir fry, on the grill, in a stew, or baked in Lasagna before you get sick of zucchini or anything that resembles it. If you're making a salad try this recipe: the Feta cheese, this helps to mask the everyday taste of zucchini. And it works!

2lbs of young and slender zucchini, medium julienne cut

Blanch in 6 cups of boiling water with 1T of salt. This particular time, you just toss it in boiling water, stir around about 10 seconds, drain and plunge in cold water immediately to stop the cooking process. This step eliminates the raw essence of zucchini.

Dressing
2 to 3 garlic cloves, crushed
3/4 t of crushed dried hot pepper flakes
1/4 cup of olive oil
1/4 cup lemon juice or vinegar
1/4 cup chopped green onion
Salt and black pepper to taste
1/2 cup of crumbled Feta cheese

Garnish
1/4 cup to 1/2 cup toasted pine nuts
Herb can be dill, Italian basil, Thai basil, or cilantro.

Squeeze out the excess moisture from blanched zucchini, in a large mixing bowl mix dressing until unified, merge in zucchini and all the fixings. Now, we have successfully abandoned the real taste (which's next to nothing) of zucchini.

Red Lentils in Salad

My husband becomes fearful every times I guzzle down this tiny but powerful little bean. However, in my defense, I don't do it to annoy anybody I simply love the taste and the fiber is just a bonus.

1cup red lentils

Dressing
1/4 cup vinegar
1/4 cup garlic oil or vegetable oil
1T soy sauce
1/2t each cayenne peppers and sugar (option)
1/2t each salt and freshly ground black peppercorns

Vegetables
1 small bell pepper, diced
Green onion for garnish
Brown mustard to taste

Pick over the lentils, wash and cook with 3 cups of water until tender to suit your taste, drain. In a medium bowl, mix the dressing until it is well blended and let it intermingle with the rest of the cast. Adjust seasoning; balance it out to suit your taste buds.

Black Bean and Corn

She stopped, peered in to the large container of bean salad.

"Wow! That's a beautiful dish, what is it?"

"It's black bean and corn salad."

"I can't have it, sorry."

"Why?" I asked with a hint of curiosity

She lowers her voice

"It's gassy! I can't stand it."

"Are you married?"

"No" She gave me a quick stare down, waiting to see where I was going with my question.

"You live alone and you are afraid to have gas? That's silly, make as much noise as you want to, it's a free country"

"Well, I actually live with someone"

"Then, even more of a reason to make extra noise."

"Actually, it's a lot of gas"

"I still stand by my statement" I said it firmly but feeling the wobbling state of the ground I was standing on I let it be. Then I wondered how much gas is a lot of gas? But anyway, with beans and corn together who needs Metamucil?

Vegetables
1 large can of black beans
2 cans vacuum packed sweet corn
1 each, red onion, green bell pepper, red bell pepper and tomato cut into small diced
1/2 cup cilantro
1-4 Jalapeno peppers, minced.

Dressing
2T olive oil
1T shallot oil
1T garlic oil
2t freshly toasted, ground cumin seed
2T sugar
1/4 cup vinegar or lime juice
Salt, pepper, chili powder to your taste

Drain beans, rinse well, do the same for corn. Put the entire diced vegetables, bean, corn, hot peppers- if use- and cilantro in a large bowl and mix well with dressing.

Serve over green lettuce Serve with sour cream and crispy tortilla chips otherwise.

Pineapple in Salad
This salad goes way back to when I first started catering. I still bring it to the market every blue moon. It's delicious with grilled chicken or pork.

1 large sweet pineapple, make sure it's ripe
1 long cucumber, the one without seed is preferred.
1 large bell pepper
Small bundle of scallions, chopped and divided
2T vegetable oil

In a large mixing bowl, cut pineapple and cucumber into bite size, do the same for pepper, toss in half of green scallions. At this point, maybe refrigerate, pour in dressing at serving time.

Dressing
Sauté the other half of scallions with oil set aside

1/4 cup light soy sauce
1T fish sauce
1/4 cup brown sugar
2T rice or white vinegar
Freshly crushed garlic
Freshly crushed hot chili

Toss dressing into pineapple mixture; don't forget to add the scallion oil. Chopped roasted peanuts may be added on top for garnish. Serve as soon as you can, because pineapple and cucumber wilt quickly.

Stanley and his Lovely Wife

A beautiful sunny morning in Bar Harbor is hard to beat when the weather is on our side and there are gorgeous people of all ages flooding the area. Very seldom do I have the time to enjoy the scenery because I'm always in action. On top of my loyal and faithful local customers I also have visitors from out of town and tourists. This story belongs to the latter.

A middle aged couple walked together (but not hand in hand). The reason they caught my eye was because the woman had such a sour look on her face while her companion seemed totally relaxed and in a browsing mode. They approached my table, stopped, and looked around from one end to another. I can always tell when a person is looking with interest or just mindlessly staring.

I noticed the man had his eyes locked onto the shrimp and avocado salad. After he circled around a couple of times, he finally found his nerve and told his wife what he wanted. Grudgingly, she snapped at him,

"I do that dish, Stanley!"

Normally, I just let things like that fly by because I do not like interfering with someone else's marital bliss. But something was very special about this lady and something drove me to express my affection towards her "sweetness". So, I scooped up a small bowl of the shrimp salad and handed it to her with a smile

"Ma'am, just looking at you I know right away you're a gourmet cook! Please have a taste and let me know if this dish is anywhere near your expectation. Criticism is more than welcome in my court."

Without hesitation she rejected my offer, "No, I don't care to try anything at all!"

"Well, I do!" Fast as a speeding bullet Stanley snatched it away from her face, dumped the whole thing in his mouth and chewed it rapidly. It only took a few seconds before he said, "May I please have a big order of this?"

Oh my God, I saw smoke pumping out of his wife's ears, because her eyes were blazing with fire. Her nostrils were flaring and with authority in her voice she hisses

"Didn't you hear what I said Stanley?"

To answer his loving wife's question: he pulled out the wallet, grasp the salad container asked for a fork and walked away. After a few steps, he turned around and looked at her. His voice was calm and unruffled,

"Joan, you might have done some sort of salad but there was no way in hell you ever made this salad! So, I'll be over there enjoying my salad." He pointed at the bench located under a shade that belongs to the YMCA garden.

What else was there for me to do except offer her a fork and a smile.

"Hurry, you still can have a taste."

She shot me a very dirty look and walked away. Are we surprised I never saw them again?

Shrimp and Avocado Salad

I dedicate this dish to a very special customer from the Bar Harbor market. He never misses a Sunday because of this particular item. One stormy day that marked the end of the year, the wind was blowing 60 mph+ for hours. There was heavy rain and it was cold and miserable. I had this salad because I knew he'd be there. But when he arrived he could only stare at an empty pan. Someone had showed up just before him and bought the whole thing. I read his disappointing eyes only too clearly and apologized. He asked, the tone of his voice was frightfully even,

"Where do they live?"

Everyone standing in line laughed, except him and his wife. She said, "He's not joking!"

I love this couple! They are the best people. I have the honor to know and to serve them food. And one thing I know without a doubt, they love me back.

Shrimp
2lbs large shrimp, peeled, deveined
2cup sea food stock or clam juice

In a large stock pan bring liquid to boil and add shrimp, when it starts to boil again, stir well for two minutes, cover pan up and turn off heat.

2 large avocado (preferred firm) cut into cubes
2 large tomatoes cut into cubes
1 medium sweet onion, sliced
1/2cup chopped fresh cilantro
1 to 5 red Jalapeno peppers, minced
Dressing
1/2 cup broth (from the cooked shrimp)
1/4 cup lime juice or vinegar

1T tomato paste
3T sugar
2t salt
3/4t black pepper
3/4t good, quality pure chili powder
2t freshly toasted and ground cumin seed
1T each garlic oil, shallot oil, pretty oil and olive oil

In a large mixing bowl, whisk dressing together, remove shrimp (save broth for later use) and toss it into dressing, gently fold in onion, avocado and tomatoes, last, but not least add herb and hot peppers.

Sarah's Shrimp Salad

We were young when we first met at our girl's preschool class. Now, her daughter has a family of her own and mine are still fancy (sort of) free. We survived everything from our kid's birthday parties to baby showers. Sometimes it is unfathomable that thirty years has just past our eyes. I still remember how she twisted her hair into a knot and secured it with a pen the very first day we met. Yes, that same hair (and mine) is gray now but our friendship stays bright and young. We don't have to see each other regularly but whenever we do, we pick it right up where we left off.

This dish reflects my friend Sarah, earthy and elegant!

Shrimp

2lbs of large shrimp, peeled deveined
3/4 t each salt, pepper and sugar
2T garlic oil or vegetable oil

Vegetables

While shrimp marinates, prepare the vegetables
2 large colored bell peppers
1 red onion
1 medium jicama

Process all the vegetables into small julienne cut and place them into a large bowl, sprinkle with 1t salt and mix well, set aside.

Dressing

1/4cup fish sauce or light soy sauce
1/4 cup broth or water
3T sugar
3T vinegar or lime juice

2T shallot or vegetable oil

Garnish
1/2cup cilantro or Thai basil
1/2cup freshly chopped roasted peanuts
Hot pepper slices and crispy shallot

Squeeze out as much as you can- the moisture from vegetables, this step is important to this dish. Simply toss and mix with dressing. Shrimp can be grilled or seared in hot skillet until no longer pink then place over vegetables, top it all off with garnish.

Chicken Salad
Chicken salad always was (and will be) a very popular item at my table for a simple reason, I work hard for it. It is a painstaking process with carefully chosen ingredients and a freshly made dressing every time. I hope the faithful customers won't be disappointed in this chapter, because I can't list all the dishes I feature at the market. This subject is big enough to carry a book by itself. Seriously!

Here, I happily share some of my favorites.

There are ways to prep the bird for salad. It all depends on how I want to present the dish. The chicken can be poached or roasted when time is not limited, marinated and grilled is definitely my choice, or pan seared for making it at the last minute.

Poaching
Immersing the whole chicken in boiling aromatic broth will deliver moist, tender, and flavorful morsels of meat. I use broth, herbs, sometimes wine and coarsely cracked pepper corn for this project. Then, I turn around and use up the liquid for soup. It's a win, win situation. The bird definitely takes something from the flavored broth but, at the same time, it will give something back as well.

Roasting
Always season the bird (or parts) inside and out before putting it in the oven and be sure to keep the skin intact for tender and moist meat. When it cools enough to touch, remove the meat from the bone, skin, and membranes before tossing it with whatever designated dressing.

To Grill
This way requires the chicken to be soaked in marinade for at least a day or two before grill time. After the meat is removed from the grill and as soon

as it's cool to your touch, shred it, and put it into action as soon as you can for the best result.

Use the same method with pan seared meat.

Poached chicken salad with shredded cabbage

Every blue moon I'll have this dish on the menu. A Vietnamese's signature! It is very simple and totally healthy. Did I mention it's also delicious? Well, I should!

To poach chicken
1 whole breast, skinless and boneless
Broth or water to cover
2t cracked coriander seed
2t cracked black peppercorns
Salt, depending on the use of water or broth

Put all the ingredients above into a medium sauce pan and bring it to a rolling boil for about ten minutes, turn off heat and cover it with couple of dish towels to retain heat.

While the chicken is cooking (by itself) prep the vegetables and the dressing. I did warn you, didn't I? Everything has to be fresh.

Vegetables
*3 cups thinly sliced white cabbage
1 cup small julienne cut carrot
1cup small julienne cut jicama
1 medium sweet onion, sliced
1/2 cup torn fresh mint

Dressing
4 large garlic cloves, crushed
1 to 4 chili peppers minced
2T each lime juice and white vinegar
3T quality fish sauce**
2 to 3T sugar***
1/4 cup shallot oil

Garnish
1/2 cup fresh roasted peanuts, chopped
Handful of fresh cilantro
Handful of crispy shallot

When the pot warms to your touch then you can remove the chicken breast, meat should be cooked and yield about 21/2 cups (hand shredding required).

In a large bowl mix chicken with dressing, gently fold in the vegetables, the last round adding the mint, lay everything down into a platter, cascade cilantro, peanuts and shallot on the top before serving.

*Fresh spring cabbages is preferred, avoid the winter storage type.

**You can use soy sauce here, it's still good; but it won't be the dish that intended to be.

*** Start with 2T, you can always add a little more to suit your taste buds, however it is hard to fix initial over seasoning. Well, you can, it just costs more work.

Lena and the Avocado salad

I was the only one in my eating club who got into this country single, the rest of them were married. By the time we were getting to know one another, they were all divorced; this is the story of how Lena got rid of her husband, or was it the other way around?

She was petite with long hair and big brown eyes. Getting married to Gerry was her one ticket to get out of Vietnam. He was a young Army sergeant and she was a barmaid. At that point in time, she saw him as a nice man who could love her and give her new opportunities. All that had changed when they settled in California. He was stuck in unemployment after getting out of the service and she was back waitressing at the Playboy club near Los Angeles. Gerry tried very hard to hold on to his wife but it didn't work. She was like a kid in a candy store and she just couldn't help herself. She wanted more and she wanted out. But Gerry was still trying to find ways to hold on to his pretty wife.

One night after closing time at the Playboy club she got home to find the front door wide open. When she entered the living room, she saw her husband's body on the floor. His face was resting against the white carpet settled in a puddle of blood. Her eyes looked around at the mess and she started to screamed, "G-d damn it! Now the carpet is ruined."

That wasn't what good old Gerry wanted to hear when he choreographed his death to test how much his wife loved him. A very messy divorce followed and Gerry moved out. Lena was fancy free just the way she wanted it.

We no longer keep in touch, but every now and then when I make chicken salad with avocado I think of her. She was nowhere near a gourmet cook but we did get to eat a lot of avocados at her house because there were several avocado trees in her back yard.

Chicken Salad and Avocado in Tequila Dressing

The chicken, our leading lady, is bathed in a Tequila marinade, fire grilled, and hand shredded then intermingled with a terrific supporting cast. All of them are happily drenched in a sinfully rich Tequila dressing. Well, it is a long way from Lena's recipe.

Meat

2 large whole chicken breasts (4halves)

With a sharp knife, start at a plump side of breast and cut it in half, you'll have 8 pieces of chicken

Wet rub for marinade

2T each pretty oil and garlic oil or 1/4c vegetables oil
2T Tequila
1/4 cup soy sauce
Juice of an orange
Juice of 1 lime
2t each cumin and good chili powder
3 garlic cloves, crushed
1t dried Oregano
1t each salt, pepper and sugar

In a large stainless steel bowl, mix chicken well into marinade. For the best result keep it in refrigerator for at least 24 hours before grilling.

Grill over medium high heat until juice running clear. When chicken is cool to touch, hand pull it into bite sizes. You'll have 5 to 6 cups of meat.

Vegetables

2 semi ripe avocados, sliced
1 large yellow bell pepper, medium julienne cut
1 medium red onion, sliced thin
2 red jalapeno peppers, chopped.
Green leafy lettuce and cilantro for garnish (option!)

Dressing

1/4 cup each chicken broth and Tequila
1/4 cup olive oil
1/4 cup lime juice or vinegar
3T agave nectar or sugar
Salt and pepper to taste

Toss grilled chicken with dressing, fold in vegetables. Lay green lettuce into the bottom of a deep large platter, mound salad on top and garnish it with herbs.

Quick Pan Seared Chicken with Sugar Pea Salad

When you see the sweet sugar snap peas appear at the farmer's market, you'll see this salad at my table. Beautiful and delicious! Too bad the sweet sugar peas never last long enough for all of us to enjoy. What about the commercially grown ones? Well, that's a different story.

Meat
4 large boneless breasts
1T crushed fresh ginger
1T crushed garlic
1t each salt and pepper
2T garlic oil or vegetable oil

Vegetables
1lb fresh sweet sugar peas, blanched in boiling water for 1 minute, chill.
1 large red bell pepper, sliced
1 can baby corn, drained

Dressing
3T rice wine vinegar
2T sweet Mirin
1/4 cup light soy sauce
1/4 cup chicken broth
2T brown sugar
2t sesame oil
2T toasted sesame seed (prefer black sesame)

With a sharp knife cut each breast into two pieces. Combine oil, ginger, garlic, salt, pepper put it all in a blender and pulse it into a paste. Rub paste all over chicken and let's it rest 2 hours in refrigerator.

Bring chicken to room temperature for a better searing task; you might want to lightly dust meat with a touch of corn starch to seal in the flavor.

In a large skillet with high heat and enough oil to lightly coat bottom pan, sear chicken until juice runs clear. Let it cool off while preparing vegetables and dressing.

Hand pull chicken into bite sizes, add vegetables and toss well with dressing, sprinkle in toasted sesame, serve at once.

The Salt Factor in Rubs

I do like rubs. It's an easy thing for those days when I don't have time to play in the kitchen. While everyday salt isn't anything fancy, I'm a little generous with the salt I use in my own rubs. The best salt to create rubs is the coarse crystal or flaky sea salt because you want to make it seem like you've fussed over it without actually fussing over it. Therefore, you need this spice to make its statement. I just cannot swallow the vision of any kind of meat being cooked without seasoning. It will never happen in my kitchen!

Flaky sea salt is full of minerals and trace elements that provide another dimension of flavor that you don't get from normal table salt, which is treated with iodine and additives.

Use a clean coffee grinder for the job and always toast spices for better flavor.

Last but not least use toasted spices as soon as you can.

Let's face it, I could give you all my recipes for rubs but you will probably go on cooking with your usual style and spices. We all have our own ways of doing things, my book or anybody else's book will not change a heck of a lot of how you go about it day to day. So, here is my two cents on the anatomy of seasoning salts.

For every tablespoon of flaky sea salt, I would use ¾ teaspoon of freshly cracked black pepper, 1/4 teaspoon cayenne pepper, 1/2 teaspoon sugar and any dried spices and herbs to suit the occasion.

That's called a spice rub.

When you take this spice rub and mix in some oil, and fresh herbs it will turn into a paste. If you take this paste and add some sort of liquid (for example: soy sauce, fish sauce, vinegar, citrus juices, or any combination thereof) you are entering the marinating territories. When I'm feeling generous, I use about 1 cup of marinade for every 2 pounds of meat but you can use more or less depending on taste. For your information: I design all my own rubs and marinades. That statement boils down to one thick fact: the food you purchase from me is one of a kind. Period!

I'm so glad we are all clear about spices, rubs, pastes and marinades. So, let's roll up our sleeves and do some serious grilling.

Summer Fare

I like women!

There used to be a BBQ place alongside the shore on the road to Bar Harbor and Northeast Harbor. Every week, four times (back and forth) I would drive by and many times I thought to stop but I never did.

One Thursday afternoon, the hunger beast roared as I approached that sign. I sold all my food and had nothing left to eat, not even one egg roll. I wanted some fuel for the drive home; there won't be time to eat at home because there's another market to prepare for. I needed to find something to eat right then. As I veered into the parking lot next to the BBQ sign I realized the whole business was operated by one man. He cooked and he served. His appearance reminded me of Mr. Clean from the commercial. I glanced at the simple menu then ordered a pulled pork sandwich.

As he handed me the food, out of habit, I made small talk.

"What kind of food- besides BBQ-do you like?"

He gave me a look then grinned, "I like women!"

I allowed the shock from his words to stun me for about five seconds, and then I turned on my best "street talking" style

"Dude, I didn't recall asking you what kind of man or woman you liked, I'm talking about food here."

He kept on grinning, his head bobbing up and down

"Yeah, I like women!"

There was a shrieking voice inside my head at that moment, and it screamed

"Run Bich Nga run!'

I turned and left and no, I didn't pay that ass. It was bad BBQ, too!

Sleeping with the Enemy

Junne was my Korean girl friend who was a member in our eating circle. Getting married to an American brought her here. The matrimony ended for both parties.

"It's just dead!" she said "I can't feel anything including sex". After her divorce, she supported herself with a waitressing job at a Disco nightclub. She was very picky when it came to men and the whole dating thing.

"I'd rather be alone and wait for however long it takes to find the right one."

It was quite sometime before her dream man entered to picture.

She gushed "I think I found Mr. Right this time."

We were all nagging to meet him but she kept saying we would have to wait for the perfect time.

One day she came home to her apartment to find that the door was already cracked open. The whole place was upside down but nothing seemed to be missing or so she thought until she walked into her bedroom. The cash tips she earned as a waitress were gone, totaling over six hundred dollars. Remember six hundred dollars was worth a lot more thirty years ago than it is today. She called the boy friend and he suggested they should call the police. He was so sweet and he stayed with her for the rest of that day. They enjoyed each other and he took her out to a fancy restaurant by the Long Beach water front. They had a nice dinner and on the way back they decided to stop at the neighborhood bar for a nightcap.

Together, they sat at the bar, the whole time he only had eyes on her. After a couple of drinks, he whispered in her ears, "How about one more round, then we'll go home for dessert?"

He got up and went to the rest room and the bartender refilled theirs drinks. She pulled out a twenty dollar bill from a pile under his glass. She immediately recognized a drawing on the corner of the bill. With just one painful look she knew exactly where the bill came from.

One of her long time admirers from the club where she waitressed always had the same question for her at the end of every night, written on every bill: "Will you get lost with me Junne?" Needless to say she was not having drinks with that admirer and realized, very quickly and painfully, who stole her money.

I guess there wasn't any point for her to show off Mr. Right to the rest of us and we didn't press.

We all liked this dish and often made a request for it whenever it was her turn to host.

Junne Fire Grilled Beef

The star of this dish is in the marinade. The cut of meat can be flank, rump, round, or tenderloin. I chose the flank steak for this particular recipe because it is easy to slice with the knife at an angle. Plus, it looks pretty and uniform when I insert the flank steak pieces onto bamboo skewers. Just don't forget to soak them first. Otherwise, make sure to grease the grill and lay the meat directly on top.

Marinade
2lbs of flank steak, slit across to 1/8 of an inch thickness
1/4 cup light soy sauce
1T dark soy sauce
2 stalks green scallion, crush with a large knife blade
2t crushed garlic
1T crushed ginger
1/2t each pepper and salt
2T brown sugar
2t sesame oil
1T garlic oil
1T hot oil

Mix marinade, add meat and toss until well coated. At this point, meat can be refrigerated from 2hr to overnight. Heat grill until hot, generously grease the grid, lay meat and spread it out, piece by piece on top of grill and cook both sides to your desired doneness.

Serve with dipping sauce, rice and pickle cabbages (see Napa cabbages)

Dipping sauce
1/4 cup light soy sauce
2T broth or water
1T vinegar
1T sugar
2T toasted and ground sesame seed
1T each crushed garlic and chili

Farewell to My Father

It always starts with a phone call. The sullen voice at the other end of the line got my attention, "Dad passed away last night". It took me a while to digest the news because I felt that he wasn't at the age to qualify visiting the final gate.

My thoughts were all about him when I was on my flight to his funeral. In his younger days, he was a professional basketball player in Vietnam. Mother still has all the pictures of him and his team mates playing the game and traveling in their fancy suits.

He was always standing tall and handsome!

When the country divided in 1954 he fled to the south with his young wife and three daughters. I was barely five years of age. That was his first voyage as a refugee.

The second voyage came along twenty two years later just before the fall of Saigon. He left two days after I did and he had to deal with the same dilemmas I endured.

Once again, my mother urged him to go without the rest of our family because she was smart; she could foresee the bigger picture.

Some may criticize and fault him in this abandoning act, others understood that by leaving my father actually had a chance to rescue them later. My parents gambled and it paid off. They reunited but not until ten years later. I was there, tears were everywhere. At that moment I couldn't keep my eyes off my mother. Her passive face told the story. Along with my father's financial help and the United States approval she still had to go through hell and back in order to get everyone out of Viet-Nam.

Here I was, standing in the front of an open casket and starring down at the finality of it all. His ashen face taunted me and made me wonder if he regretted not saying the thousand of words he had never said to his children, or the thousands of things he took for granted from my mother. I don't know, for we are all victimized by our own culture.

I touched his face for the last time, choking on my good bye words. The ceremony lasted three days before the cremation process took place. Hundreds of guests each picked their own flower and placed them around him in his coffin but only the immediate family members were allowed by his side during the final steps inside the cremation room.

Inside the room I was peeking into the flicker of fire which waited to fulfill its job. Suddenly a vision of a little girl on the back of a motor bike with her father driving her to school came into my mind. She was clutching his waist because the wind and rain was beating down on them. How vivid that memory was playing in my head at that moment and I had not thought about in forever. The casket became slowly engulfed by the fire and I watched as my mother collapsed into her oldest son's arms.

A Few Steak Dinners for My Dad

My father loved Western food: steak and potatoes. I think it was a result of years of working with the people from UNICEF. There were times he brought home butter, ham, and imported stinky French Fromage (no surprise here, France produces 240 plus different kinds of cheeses). I've known all of those items from a very young age and that's not normal when you are growing up in Viet Nam.

I observed my mother cooking steak for Dad countless times. My mother possesses a great skill in the kitchen and the woman can cook just about anything, much less a piece of beef in the frying pan. So, she repeats the same dish with a lot of twists and turns, only for him! The rest of us we don't get to eat steak, if we were lucky we got some water buffalo meat for stir fry, occasionally!

Here are a few more steak dinners for my Dad. It's has my mother's technique imprinted on it but the tastes are all mine. I hope great journeys are waiting for him, to wherever his heart desires to go.

Meat
2lbs of Rib-eye steak (4 pieces) 1/2 inch thick
2T minced garlic
1t each salt and coarse black peppers
1T garlic oil

Rub steaks with garlic, salt, pepper and brush with garlic oil, set aside.

Sauce
1/2 cup red wine
1/2 cup beef broth mixed with 1t cornstarch
1T soy sauce
8 oz mushroom, sliced.
8oz baby spinach, washed, dried.

Divide spinach equally onto 4 dinner plates
In a large, nonstick skillet and high heat, drizzle in just enough oil for a thin coat, cook steak to medium rare- about 3 to 4 minutes each side- Remove from skillet, cover and keep warm.
Back to skillet, add red wine and deglaze pan, drizzle in a bit more oil as needed. Let the wine boil down a little more before adding mushrooms and broth together with soy sauce. This process shouldn't take more than few minutes.
Lay each cooked steak over the serving plate with the baby spinach; pour the bubbling sauce to top it all. Serve at once with crispy French fries on the side.

Spicy Grilled Beef with Lemongrass

Everybody can throw a piece of steak on top of the grill. However, if you want to impress your guests then you'll have to go the extra mile. Leftovers of this dish make the best sandwiches.

2lbs flank steak cut across to 1/8 of an inch

Paste
In food processor, pulse,
2 stalks of lemongrass, sliced thin
4 cloves of garlic

1/2t turmeric powder
Fresh jalapeno to your taste
1/4 cup fish sauce
2T sugar
1/2t each salt and pepper
1T each garlic and onion oil
Hot oil if desired

Grill as previous beef dish, serve with your favorite steamed vegetables, rice and dipping sauce. If you want to be more authentic, sprinkle chopped roasted peanuts on top of beef before serving can be teamed it up with rice noodles, lettuce, and cucumber; top it with herbs like mint, cilantro and Siam queen basil for a special summer salad.

Spicy dipping sauce
3 cloves of garlic crushed
Hot peppers to your taste
3T sugar
1T lime juice
2T water
1T white vinegar
1/4 to 1/3 cup of fish sauce, depending of the brand used

The Bad Boy— T-bone steak
There are few things in life that need not be disturbed or interfered with. The flavor of a T-bone steak is one of them. This cut of steak is my favorite over the grill. I use cheap steak all the time to play with all kind of marinades and different spices and all sorts of rubs. The finished product that comes out with a fantastic result always makes me feel like I got away with murder, but, when I use a piece of good, quality steak then simplicity is the only ingredient I need.

This is all you'll need: coarse sea salt, freshly ground pepper, a hefty pinch of pure Chili powder, a lighter pinch of cayenne pepper, a touch of thyme and garlic.

Don't forget to brush the steak with garlic oil-or olive oil- patting seasoning over it and throw that baby into the top of a roaring grill. If life is not perfect, when you put that piece of meat in your mouth it will be!

To me, it's seems too sinful for this act to be repeated continuously. How special can it be if I do it all the time? My husband might say otherwise.

Grilled Steak in Ginger and Wine Dressing
2 New York strips steak, approximately 2lbs, cut each steak into three pieces

Marinade
1/4 cup beef broth*
2T light soy sauce
2T rice wine
2T brown sugar
1T crushed ginger
1T garlic oil
2t sesame oil

In a medium size of stainless steel bowl, toss meat into marinade, mix well and let it rest from 2hours to overnight.

In the summer, please use the outdoor grill. The broiler will do the job, but it will not make a memory. The famous boxer grill will also do the job, only if you desperate.

I suggest after spending a good amount of money for two good steaks, some more for wine, ginger, and soy sauce not to mention your time and effort to make the garlic oil, please grill it over a hot coal and baste it constantly. Avoid overcooking beef.

*If you don't have good homemade stock, choose the one from the can carefully.

Water is better than bad broth any day!

My "Famous" Neighbors
Once upon a time, I moved to Winterport from a small town named Corinna. Believe me, Winterport is no bigger and I know for certain because I've lived at this spot of town longer than the people around me. Throughout this story, I'll explain the reason why my current neighbors are famous (to me).

I read somewhere that if more than two hundred people know you, then, you're famous. On one side, I have Kay, she's a professor, so I'm sure over the years of teaching it is not a problem for Kay being labeled as famous with all her students.

Rose Fisher used to tend to more than one farmer's market every week before she retired. So, I'm positive two hundred is a small number to nail Rose as famous. The guy on the other side is a very funny man, but he told me he doesn't like anybody. He is not even sure if he likes the man (his friend) I married but he likes me. That's entitles him to be famous in my book.

The lady next door is well known to anybody who watches the morning's news on television so of courses she's famous.

That's all I'm going to say about my current neighbors.

This story is about the people who lived in the house before the television lady. Although the couple who used to be there were not famous, their best friend was legendary. I mean this guy is known globally, he's a writer from in Bangor.

When we met this famous writer he was visiting my neighbor, his college roommate. The writer tried his hardest to act like "Oh, I'm just one of you". Yeah, I don't think so.

Anyway, this tale is not about him. I was young when our old neighbors were there. We were close and our children were young. We did things together like play games, share dinners, and then one sad day they moved away from us. Time flies the children grow up, and being busy with our lives, we drifted apart.

Then one day, we received an invitation to celebrate their only child graduating from high school. I was excited! We hadn't seen these people for at least fifteen years.

The big celebration event was held outside, someone was grilling, and a wonderful aroma filled the yard. Sally greeted us with open arms and there were tears in our eyes when we embraced. We walked alongside a long table flooded with food. There were lots of salad and pasta dishes with a huge platter of grilled steak as a center piece. I was pointing out how different we were (grayer, more wrinkles) as I dished out my plate. After biting into a piece of steak I was completely impressed

"Sally, this is good! Since when you've learn how to cook like this? Things have changed big time."

She gave me a shove with her elbow; her eyes narrowed, "Nothing has changed; you still like your own food! That's your recipe and it has been famous in my house since the day you gave it to me." I had completely forgotten about that.

Sate for the Grill

I used to grill a lot of Sate in the summer while the kids were growing up, and a lot of times I do it for catering jobs. Making small pieces of meat on skewers and grilling them is a tedious job. But, if you have a little time and don't mind a bit of work, believe me; you can't find better tasting meat anywhere.

Meat

1 large pork tenderloin sliced across1/2 inch thick. Approximately 1 dozen slices.
1 large boneless chicken breast, sliced across to 1/2 inch thick slices, about 1 dozen.

Soak 24 wooden skewers into water. I often use the stainless steel type for this task

Marinade
In a large mixing bowl whisk together
1cup coconut cream
1t salt
1t black pepper
1/4 cup light soy sauce
2t ground coriander seed
2T freshly crushed ginger
2T finely minced shallot
Hot chili paste to your taste.

Insert meat into bamboo skewer, divide marinade into two containers-one for pork, the other chicken- Pour half dressing over chicken. Add 1t toasted, ground cumin seed to the other half of dressing going into the pork. Make sure the meat is bathed all around with dressing. Rest this, in the refrigerator from 2 hours to overnight

Dipping sauce
3 large cloves garlic, crushed
2T vegetable oil
1cup coconut cream (now, you'll use up the whole can)
1/4 cup chicken broth
1cup smooth peanut butter
2-3T fresh squeezed lime juice
2T fish sauce or soy sauce
2T hot pepper paste
1/4 cup of brown sugar

In a small sauce pan with oil, sauté garlic until fragrant, add the broth and the rest of the ingredients, stir and bring all to boil. Remove from heat, let it cool.

Grill meat until juice runs clear; enjoy it with the dipping sauce.

Cubes of cucumber and rice would make a good accompaniment to this dish

Baby in the Cornhusk

The summer Lily and I left the city for a weekend to get away was a memorable one. It was midday when we arrived at our destination and the air was hot, thick, and humid. The small cottage with three rooms was located at the end of a winding dirt road, and I complained to Lily how isolated and eerie the place was.

Giving me one of her famous smirks she chuckled, "Isn't that the whole idea of getting away?" Then, she explained, "My cousin and her husband own this place, they live right next door". She made a circling gesture with her arms, "but we have to walk a bit of a distance to get there, but that's where dinner is going to be served". She sauntered toward the next room and I could hear her trailing footsteps.

I was uncomfortable and I remembered thinking to myself "I hope I don't pass out from this heat". I was agitated because I don't like to be hungry and too hot or too cold. I looked toward the front door just to make sure it was wide open for air and that's when I thought I saw a person.

She was walking in slow motion. It wasn't as if what I was seeing was only her; I saw her arms cradling a naked baby and cornhusks. I was not sure about the cornhusks at that moment but I was positive that I saw her teary eyes and because she looked right at me I noticed her head was shaved.

In the middle of the intense heat I felt all the hairs on my neck stand up and a wisp of chilled air run right through them.

I screamed to the next room where I could hear the sound of Lily unpacking.

"Lily, come here, right now!"

"What in the world are you yelling at?" Lily was annoyed as she has a very short temper.

I turned around to face Lily then pointed at the front door

"We have visitor"

We both looked out: nobody in sight. There's no freaking way she could have gone anywhere. I told Lily what I saw and we both walked outside. The small dirt road led to the dead end cottage which was covered on both sides with local foliage and old thick bamboo bushes. "Where'd she go?" I wondered.

"You need to lie down and take a nap." Lily said impatiently.

"Listen, she looked right at me, she carried a naked baby in her arms and she was crying"

Then I pointed my finger at her, "By the way, let me tell you she had no hair. Zip! Bald as honey dew"

"Then where is she?"

I couldn't answer that any more than I could accept her accusing me of hallucinating. She winked and tapped my shoulder before she walked away. It's so Lily!

"Just blame it on the heat."

Later that evening we were having dinner with the folks that owned the place. I told them about what I saw and I had the sheer pleasure of witnessing Lily's eyes pop out when the woman grinned to me.

"She let you see her. She likes you!"

Her smile widened.

"Oh! She's legendary around here. My husband sees her from time to time but I never did. Tenants come and go. Most claim they hear her cry but very few people see her with the baby. She died giving birth to a stillborn boy years ago," she paused and pointed her finger to the distance out of the side window, "In the corn field, not that far from here"

Now, I understood the puzzle of the cornhusks.

Great Corn inside the Husk

Every summer I tend to get a bit rounder at the midriff because of my lust for fresh corn. You can't go wrong no matter how you cook it. If I'm in a lazy mood, I just throw it in a pot of boiling water and cook for 6 minutes. There is also fresh corn pudding and fritters. The list can go on and on. If I have the grill going and the corn is ready to be picked in the garden, I have to cook this side dish. I have to cook at least 12 ears, because six of them belong to me.

12 ears of fresh corns

Sauce
1/4 cup vegetable oil
1 bunch of scallions coarsely chopped
1t each salt and sugar
1/4 cup Mirin wine
1/4 cup light soy sauce

In a small saucepan with oil, add scallions and cook until bubbling, about one minute, remove from heat, add the rest of the ingredients mix well, set aside.

Soak fresh corn in cold water for 30 minutes

Pull husk down, away from corn but don't break it off, clean all the silk out, use a pastry brush and brush a light coat of sauce into every ear. Pull husk back and set it directly on grill. Set heat to medium, cover, cook for 6 to 8 minutes, turn, cook another five minutes on the other side. Remove from grill and remove husk, set corn back to grill and cook just enough to lightly char all around. Set corns over a deep serving platter, drizzle the rest of sauce over each and every ear and enjoy!

Make 12 servings for normal people. Make 2 for me.

Tip for corn

No summer barbecue is worth having unless there's fresh corn on the menu and of course there's no better place to buy your corn other than your local farmers market. You have the choice of varieties, for instance if you like the taste of old fashioned sweet corn you might want to try the "butter and sugar" type. I, myself love the golden one; I like the crunch in my corn kennel, and this type of corn sure does deliver it. For late in the season, try the Silver Queen type.

Just because you buy your vegetables at your farmers market don't assume they are always fresh. Know your corn, pick the one that's plump and has fresh husks with dark tipped tassels.

Last, but not least, examine the parts where the ear connects to the plant, making sure they still have the moisture without any discoloring. Eating well sure takes lots of work, but I'm a willing slave for my love of corn.

Sweet Treats

The Out of Town

When the leaves start to change color I would see him back in town. So, for the next four Sundays mornings, I would have a chance to serve him his favorite dishes along with some enjoyable conversation. No topic out of the ordinary: food in general, weather, sometimes even political banter would take place, then the usual goodbye when he had to go back to where he came from.

"I'll see you next year" he would say.

"I hope so, have a good year and be well," was my usual reply,

Then came one year when he added another line to his routine

"By the way, I think you are very sexy" he said with a broad grin.

A shock ran through my body. Where in the world did that come from? But, as smooth as coconut custard over sweet and spicy ginger caramel sauce, I laughed "Hell yes, that's the line my husband keeps telling me."

But, after thirty years, if he really did say that I'd drop dead.

Creamy Coconut Custard and Ginger Caramel over Delicata Squash

This is a dessert that has plenty of benefits, tastes included.

Caramel

1/2 cup light brown sugars
1/2 cup of hot water
2T crushed ginger root

For the custard

1 can of coconut milk
4 large eggs
1/3 cup sugar
1t vanilla
1/2t salt
4 medium- large Delicata squashes

Heat oven to 350 degrees

Clean squash, cut each one lengthwise in half, and scoop out all the seeds and membranes. Trim the inside, so it can hold up to three and half - four cups of liquid.

Use a peeler and run it across the bottom of each half, this step will help to provide a stable ground when situating squash on the baking sheet.

Partially cook squash in microwave oven with high heat from 8 to 10 minutes. While squash is cooking, make your caramel. With high heat, bring sugar to boil along with ginger, stir constantly and watch it like a hawk. When sugar turns to a beautiful amber color, immediately pour in the boiling water, keep stirring and lower the heat. Caramel will be ready when it becomes lightly thick and aromatic. Keep warm.

Carefully remove squash from the microwave oven, feel squash's texture. It's should be almost tender but firm. Divide caramel over squash, tilt it to coat well, careful not to burn yourself. Lay squash over a large, oven proof baking sheet.

Pour coconut into a microwave safe bowl and scald for three to four minutes. Coconut should be very hot but not boiling. Beat eggs with sugar and vanilla, fold in hot coconut and pour mixture into squash. Bake in preheated oven for 40+ minutes until custard is set. The best thing about this kind of squash is that you can eat the whole thing, you might use other squash such as sweet dumpling, acorn or carnival but then you will have to avoid the skin.

I like warm custard, others might disagree.

Happy Food

By now, if you are reading this far then you know that I love sugar for my tofu and ginger. It's always the leading choice for flavor. So, what happens when all three ingredients intermingle in one place as a dessert? Well, sadly I couldn't think of it on my own but I did receive some help. The first time when she stopped at my door, I was beyond shocked by her appearance. She was barely five feet tall yet half of her frame was forced toward the ground from a deformed backbone. A lump, as big as a basket ball, caused her initial form to look like she had two heads. I couldn't believe she was able to carry her whole operation which consisted of two large big pots, dishes, all balanced by a wooden stick over her shoulder. I knew right away she was one of the vendors who traveled around to selling food. That's how it was back then in Viet Nam, you didn't have to cook, better yet, you didn't even have to get out of the house to shop. You could purchase food right at your door, you name it, from soups to entrées and sweet treats around the clock. No wonder I have a weight issue.

"Miss, would you like to try some tofu in sweet ginger sauce?" she asked with a smile.

"Is that what you are selling?" I was genuinely surprised by her coming to my door with a question, because food vendors didn't usually do that.

"Well, I hope you don't mind that I stopped by and offered ..." As if she could read my mind.

"No, I don't mind. But, dessert with tofu, I'm afraid I just don't see the connection"

"Give it a chance, it really is delicious!"

So, she set the whole process down at my front door, quickly got a hold of a small bowl from the back, grasped a sharp flat spoon, open the steaming hot pot at the front. Then with a swift motion sliced and scooped out the creamy silken tofu, layer and layer almost to the rim. She closed the pot and turned around and topped the tofu with golden fragrant syrup, inserted a small spoon and handed it to me. I was just mesmerized at how efficiently she pulled everything together. She flashed an ear to ear smile,

"Here, taste, if you don't like it you don't have to buy it"

It was love at the first spoon, not only did I become her regular customer from then on, I paid in advance every week. Around three o'clock, I'd meet her at the door with my own bowl, and then we'd start to talk, each time longer than before.

There are people out there born just for the purpose of irritating the day-lights out of whoever happens to be closed by. And then there are some people- special, to say the least- that possess an aura of happiness that's hard not to catch when they are around you. This street vendor totally belonged to the second category.

I learned she was born deformed from some sort of bone disease, which encouraged the extra growth to her back. She lived in the small hut with her mother on the other side of town, her father died in the war when she was very young. When she talked about her mother her face lit up, when she discussed her neighbors her voice was full of affection. I was blown away from the kind light I saw as her spirit. Once I asked if she had a boy friend. She laughed, shook her head and pointed to her back. She had a name for it and comfortably embraced it.

I noticed she didn't have much clothing so I would gather some of mine then went around and collected extra from the women at work. I spotted a tear in her eyes when she reached in and pulled out a shirt, admired it, but then said it might be too fancy for her to wear.

She giggled as she wore it the next day. Never underestimate the power of a pretty blouse.

Then one day, I just got home after my hair appointment and I spotted her waiting for me. Just her alone without the whole kitchen she usually carried over her shoulder, and she was beaming

"I come just to say goodbye, my aunt will take over this route, you'll still get your tofu, she's very excited and she can't wait to meet you"

"Is something wrong with you?" I tried to keep my voice even.

"Everything is right!" She was glowing "I'm getting married, can you believe that? I'm so lucky! Someone actually wants me"

I took her hand, seriously looking into her eyes and said it sincerely,

"You are a beautiful person! He's the lucky one and don't you ever let him forget that"

Over a year later, after coming home from a business trip, my maid told me I had a visitor while I was away- a young woman with a baby and she paused.

"She left a message for you". I turned my head, puzzled with no idea what it was,

"What'd she say?"

"She remembers to remind her husband he's the lucky one!"

I can still hear myself laughing. There were times in my life when the wind blew some bad things my way, but instead allowing myself to drown in sorrow I try to think of her and I can almost see her face as she tilts her head back and rests it on top of her second one, then grinning and proclaiming, "Bet you can't do that!"

She's right! The only thing I can do is try to imitate the memory of this dish which she introduced to me years ago. I have to confess, if this desert was bad for me, I still couldn't help myself.

Creamy Silken Tofu in Ginger Syrup
Silken tofu
1/2 cup dried soy beans
2T rice flour
1T gypsum powder mixed well with 1t water

Syrup
A large piece of fresh ginger (as your thumb) crushed
1 cup brown sugar
1 and 1/4 cup water

Wash and soak the soybeans overnight. Drain well.

In the blender with 3 cups of water, puree the soy beans for few minutes, and then pour it over a strainer lined with cheesecloth. Catch the drippings with a stock pot.

Gathering all corners of cloth, tightly squeeze out the milk into pot and return pulp back to blender, adding 3 more cups of water and do it all over again.

Add rice flour to soy milk, mix until it is well blended and bring it to boil. Watch it like a hawk so it won't boil over, stirring constantly so it won't stick to the pot and burn.

When you spot a lot of foam on the surface; that means it is almost boiling, lower heat at this point and let it simmer for two to three minutes. Turn off heat.

Ladle about 1/2cup of hot milk over the gypsum powder mixture, blend thoroughly and quickly pour it back to the milk pot, stir well then cover pot tightly, let it jell and don't disturb. It will take about 30 minutes, time to make the syrup.

In a medium sauce pan with syrup ingredients, bring to a gentle boil for few minutes. Turn off heat, let steep.

The creamy silken tofu should be served layer upon layer of thin slices. Lay three parts of tofu in a dessert bowl; pour in one part of hot syrup and serve it warm.

When I don't have time to go through all the fuss, I would pick up a package of silken tofu-yes, store bought one- and serve it with the same syrup as described. While it's not the real thing, it still makes me happy.

*Gypsum powder can be found at a health food store or Oriental market. Add it is a chemical agent used to coagulate soybean milk.

Tropical Fruit Salad for Dessert

Here, I'll share a dessert I believe will benefit your health as much as your taste buds.

1 fully ripe mango, peeled and cut into cubes
1 fully ripe papaya, peeled, seed removed and cut into bite size
2 kiwi peeled cut into 8 pieces
1 can of lychee, drained save the juice in the freezer
2 passion fruits
Juice of 1 lime, save the green rind
Honey to sweeten (only if needed)

Cut passion fruit in half, scoop out the seeds and put it in a strainer, set strainer over a bowl and press seeds down to release the juice. This step can be done a day ahead.

Combine the passion fruit juice, lime with the green rind and honey. Break up the frozen lychee syrup, and whisk in the fruit juice. Pour over the cut up fruit and serve.

Garnish with mint for special effect.

Berries Beauty
Guilt free treats.

1 fresh pineapple, clean out all brown eyes and cut into cubes
4 cups of strawberries, halved
2 cups blueberries
2 cups blackberries
1 can of Mangosteen, drained, juice reserved*

Dressing
1/4 cup white rum
Reserved juice from Mangosteen
Honey to taste
Lemon juice for added tang

In a small stainless steel bowl, whirl dressing so the ingredients can blend in harmony, adjust taste before setting the bowl with dressing in freezer for at least two hours.

Just before serving, break dressing to slush and spoon it all over berries.

*For a fancier effect, when you hollow out the pineapple, use a curved knife for tool and carefully lift the meaty part out; use the two shells for center piece. Scatter few small dessert bowls around it and fill them all up with the colorful berries.

*You can easily find Mangosteen at any special food store or Asian market.

Sunshine Mango Custard with Gorgeous Raspberry Sauce
This healthy desert says it all!

2 ripe mangoes, peeled, seeded, puree and set aside.

For custard
4 egg yolks
1/4 cup sugar
3T cornstarch
Pinch of salt
2t vanilla
1cup coconut cream, divided

In a medium bowl, mix the egg yolks, sugar; add the corn starch, salt, vanilla with 2T coconut milk until well blended and smooth. Bring the rest of coconut cream to a soft boil, then, slowly pour in the mixture of custard, cook over low heat and stir constantly until sauce thickens Turn heat off.

Immediately add the puree mango, mix to well blend. Allow to cool.

Raspberry sauce
3 cups raspberry pick a few pretty ones and set them aside for garnish.
3T sugar

Simmer berries in sugar for about one minute, remove seeds through a strainer. Allow to cool off.

To serve: Divided sauce and custard over 4 to 6 different serving dessert dishes, make each into 2 separated pools. Decorate custard side with reserved berry, use tip of a knife and swirl raspberry sauce over custard's edge. Chill until ready to serve.

For color effect, garnish with fresh mint.

Fried Banana for Dessert
If you are a regular customer to any Vietnamese restaurant, you'll be familiar to this dish. Nothing fancy, just a good old banana dipped into a light batter and fried until golden brown. You'll usually have the option to flambé it with rum, then drizzle it with some caramel sauce. That's fine and dandy but the way I look at, it's already delicious the way it is, who needs all the extra calories?

4 to 5 large bananas
Corn starch for dusting

Batter
1cup of all purpose flour
2T cornstarch
2T potato starch
1 1/2t baking powder
1T sugar
Good pinch of salt
1cup of iced cold water
Vegetable oil for fry

In medium bowl combine flour and its supporting cast, make a well in the center and whisk in cold water to make a smooth paste. Refrigerate it for an hour.

Cut each banana into 4 pieces, dust them with cornstarch- this step is an insurance policy for crispier result- In a wok, or heavy deep skillet pour in about 2inches of oil, heat oil up to 375 degrees, dip banana into batter a few pieces at a time, fry until golden, turn once. Present them prettily in a large serving platter.

To flambé

Use approximately 1/2cup of good rum, pour rum in a ladle then ignite it into a flame, gently pour this fire over the crispy banana, make sure they coat well for the best alcohol effect. Dust with powdered sugar if desired and serve it immediately. I usually can't keep my hands off the first one fresh from the sizzling oil. Cook has priorities.

Pudding in the Rain

When I left the Buck Street to join the Orono Market, the move created a little stir. Most customers eventually followed me to the new place while only a few resented my move and crossed me out. Here, I would like to take this opportunity to say that the move was the best decision we've made. It was the right time to move on.

For the loss of a few, I've gained so much more and not just in customers. This market has more than thirty vendors and it's set alongside a river, so for most of the summer, the breeze is always a welcome pleasantry to all of us.

The customers here are the most loyal people on earth and not just to me. The rest of the vendors would have to agree with me. I felt comfortable and at ease at my new home from the very first day. With the change in address I designed a different menu. This dessert used to be a regular at the previous market but now I've dropped it altogether and never looked back.

Three summers later, over a special occasion when all my girls were at home, I made it and took some to Orono. It was a rainy day and I had so many regular items, there wasn't any room to feature the dessert so the pudding lay lonely in the back of the car. As I was looking at it, I immediately thought of one certain lady. She used to regularly come to the Buck Street market but I hadn't seen her once since my move. She always loved this item and I was thinking "Wow, only if she knew". At that exact moment, I looked up, there she was in a dripping rain coat and my jaw dropped. When I finally found my words, it was almost like something got caught in my throat,

"Can you believe I have your favorite dessert?"

"No way, I don't believe it!" Her eyes opened wide with awe.

"I haven't made this dish in years" I confessed. She wanted to know why.

"I really don't know" I shook my head.

"Well, this is my lucky day!" She said.

"No, it's my fortune; I haven't see you in forever"

That was the only time I've ever seen her in Orono, the solitary time this dessert made it to the new market. The first and last pudding in the rain!

Banana with Tapioca Pearl and Coconut

*2lbs banana, oriental type but the regular store brands will do
1/2 cup water

2T small pearl Tapioca
1/2 cup of sugar
1/4t salt
1 can of coconut milk
1/4 cup toasted sesame seed, ground and mixed with 1/2t salt. Do this part ahead and set it aside for the garnish.

Peel banana, cut in half crosswise, and then cut again lengthwise.

In a medium sauce pan, bring water and tapioca to boil then lower heat and cover with lid. Simmer for 10 minutes then add sugar, salt and banana, then cook for another 10 minutes stir in coconut. Bring it to a soft boil and remove from heat.

Serve warm, sprinkle with toasted reserved sesame seeds

*Around here, the only oriental banana I can find is in the can, use 2 cans and slice banana into four slices.

Claudia

I can't have a cookbook to celebrate friendship without the mention of my sister-in-law

Claudia. Even if we weren't married to two brothers we could easily be each other's BFFs. Although we both love food she's the one with zero body fat in contrast to me whose is round and plump all over. Recently we took a vacation together and had a fantastic time. For a week we dined out every night. I let my evil fat twin jump out of me and go wild with desserts. Claudia was doing the same thing. At the end of the week it made no difference to her waist line but I was suffering the consequences. I didn't just gain weight I did worse- I gained inches.

By the fourth day of the week, she complimented me on a pretty skirt I was wearing. I just let the woman say her peace before I said mine.

"Claudia, you've seen the good looking outside, now, let me show you the ugly inside."

Gingerly I lifted up my blouse to show off the zipper which couldn't make it to the top of the skirt. I had to press it down alongside my growing hips. The woman laughed so hard, you would think she'd witnessed a great comedy act. I just let her have her fun.

Later that night, while we were going over the menu she asked the waiter which one was low fat (as usual). He recommended the short rib confit, so Claudia jumped right in and devoured it, gushing about how good it was. Now, it was time to have my fun.

"Claudia dear, do you know why that dish was so good? Why it's so smooth?"

"Oh yes, very tender too"

I'm grinning ear to ear now.

"You know when you're shopping at the beef section and you see the package of ribs with fifty percent bone, forty five percent fats and merely five percent meat barely clinging to it, that's called a short rib. The term "confit" means slow braising in its own fat. Now, you know why it's so smooth. It doesn't matter anyway; you do need to put on some fat to catch up with me. Payback time"

The sad part is I can go on and diet until the cows come home, but I still can't have her tiny waist. It will just never happen. I'll be portly to the end of time, that's my destiny!

Claudia loves the sweet potatoes with cassava root below. I'm holding a grudge over the fact she can eat the whole pan and it doesn't show up on her waistline.

Sweet Potatoes with Cassava Root

Here, I would like to share with you one of my all times favorite sweet treats. It's wheat free and dairy free. But, please don't judge the simplicity of the ingredients and cross it out, it really is delicious. On top of that, you'll get the bonus of protein from Mung beans and sweet potatoes.

1cup of dried Mung beans, rinsed.
1/2 cup diced dried Cassava root*
5 cups water
2 cups diced sweet potatoes
1 cup light brown sugar
1 can of coconut milk
1/2t salt
1t vanilla

In a medium sauce pan, combine the first three ingredients and bring to boil, stir to break up the Cassava root, turn off heat, keep lid tight and let it rest for an hour.

Add sweet potatoes and sugar; bring it to boil again and simmer about ten minutes. Pour in coconut milk, stir, when it's almost to boiling point add salt and vanilla then remove from heat.

In the winter, serve it as a warm dessert.

In the middle of summer heat, serve chilled.

Can't eat it all, freeze by portion for later enjoyment.

*Dried Cassava root can be found at special food stores. Large tapioca pearl can be substituted for the Cassava root. You just have to adjust the cooking time for tapioca.

White People Food

My daughter Sara refers to every other dish I put on the table that's not exotic as "white people food". So here in this chapter I would like to share my family favorite versions of Western cuisine.

From my last book, she was the one who graduated from Tufts University, paid her dues to the United States Navy and served her country in South America and Iraq. She's now enjoying her civilian life, away from Maine, but often enough she calls with questions. If it's for me it's most likely about food or the garden, every other issue belongs to her father. Funny enough, this is the same person who was terrified every time we made her go out to help in the garden, now she's growing her own vegetables.

Sometimes, the phone would ring in the middle of the day,

"Mom, I got invited to a pot luck dinner and I don't know what to bring"

"What do you have in the pantry?

"Just some pasta"

"Make a Capri style pasta salad with whatever vegetables you got, all you have to do is created a killer dressing then all eyes will be on you, guaranteed!"

I can tell that my daughter was getting excited now.

"Oh, oh, I got fresh basil in the garden and tomatoes. I even have a ball of fresh Mozzarella cheese. This salad's going to be good! Mommy, you are so smart."

Sara is the only one of my kids who addresses me as Mommy and I love it!

"Don't be stingy with the olive oil or the fresh grated Parmesan cheese," my advice to her as she says her goodbye.

"There goes another dish of white people's food you are going to make Sara."

And she always laughs at my reminder.

Meatball for other Occasions

I'm so spoiled when it comes to food, not just with Far East food but every other kind. For instance, I can't hack the kind of frozen meatballs that I've seen people buy. Those meatballs are sold by the big bag at the local food club. I'm positive it's not the taste that draws the sales. Believe me I sampled them one time and I won't be doing it again.

I would like to share my meatballs and you can compare.

1 cup bread crumbs (homemade preferred) from day old French bread.
1/4 cup beef broth
In small bowl soak bread crumbs with broth, set aside.
1lb of ground chuck
1lb of ground pork*
1/3 cup minced sweet onion
2T minced garlic
1T hot peppers flake (option)
1t each salt and black pepper
3/4 cup fresh grated Pecorino Romano chesses
2 eggs

In a large mixing bowl combine all the ingredients above and gently blend them in together, you'll have a tough meat balls otherwise.

Pick up a handful of the mixture, using the squeezing motion; and scoop it up with the spoon off the top of your thumb and index finger, this method will produce a same size of meat ball every time.

Always use a large skillet with heavy bottom for the browning task.

Now it's now ready to be incorporated with whatever sauce is its destination. Tomatoes for spaghetti, white sauce, cheese sauce etc...

Omit the cheese then add ginger and nutmeg if you want to use it for Swedish meat balls instead.

*Sometimes I use the pork with garlic sausage from my colleague at the Corners Stone farm instead of ground pork, this is one out of few reasons I'm not a vegetarian.

Mac and Cheese

My youngest daughter Sam loves macaroni and cheese. This is how I usually go about making this dish, Sam loves it and that's all that matters to me.

1lb of macaroni
1/2lb of Monterey Jack cheese, cut into small cubes.
1/2lb of sharp chipotle cheddar cheese, cut into small cubes
4T butter
1/4 cup flour
2 cup stock or, 1 can of broth
12 oz can of evaporated milk

Salt and pepper to taste
Panko bread crumbs to top (option)

Turn oven to 350 degree.

Cook macaroni for about 5 to 6 minutes, drain, set aside

In a deep large skillet, melt butter slowly, whisk in flour and when it starts to bubble add milk and broth, keeping the whisking motion going while adding cheese, bring it all to melt.

Stir in the reserved macaroni, seasoning with salt and pepper to your taste. Depending on the brand of cheese you are using, lots of time I don't even bother with the salt at all.

Top it with Panko bread crumbs and place it in the preheated oven for 45 minutes.

Serve it with pickled Jalapeno peppers for a good kick. Crispy bacon crumbs will be on top if I'm in a generous (with the fat) mood.

B.B.Q Ribs

This is one out of the few reasons I could never turn myself into a vegetarian. I love a honking piece of spicy pork baby back ribs, rubbed in all kinds of spices, wrap it up tightly and throw it in 350 degree oven until tender: approximately 2 hours. The task does not end there. Unwrap it then fire grill it until it's crispy all over. The best part is still yet to come because after all that I'll drench it with sweet, spicy, tangy sauce. Who can resist ribs? Not me.

1 whole rack of pork rib (or baby back) from 5 – 7 lbs.

Wash, rinse and dry with paper towel

Rub
2T coarse salt
2T brown sugar
2t paprika, the smoky type is preferred here
1T coarse black pepper corn
1T hot pepper flakes, more for me personally.
1T granulated dried garlic
1T onion powder
A touch of celery seed powder
Cayenne peppers to your taste

Start at the meaty' side and generously rub it with spices, let your finger do the patting Cover; let rest from 2hrs to overnight, no longer than that!

If you have a smoker, turn it to 225 degree and it will take approximately 4 hours for the task. Charcoal grill; you got to set up the grill for indirect grilling, adjust the vent hole to keep temperature around 325 degree and grill from 1- 1/2 to 2 hrs.

Gas grill, do what I suggest earlier.

Sauce
1cup tomato based smoky BBQ sauce
1/2 cup tamarind pulp extracted*
2T soy sauce
1/2 cup honey
1/4 cup dark brown sugar
Hot pepper sauce to your desire

*Tamarind pod is sold at natural food stores in dry form of a block. For every 8oz block, extract with 2 cups of boiling water and strain it through a sieve. This item freezes well (place it in ice cube maker) wrap tightly, multiple uses in sauces, curry etc…

Why do I choose this item for tanginess? When you need a bit of exotic in your sour; this is a good candidate for the job. Not all sour is created equal!

As much as I cook all the time, I still am in a learning process, at least, that where I see myself: an undereducated cook. I'll get there someday, as long as I do not stop learning.

Coleslaw
What kind of BBQ ribs could you have if you don't have a good old American slaw on the side? We love all kind of coleslaw in our house and this particular one is designed for the ribs.

1 head of fresh spring cabbage cut up. This should make about 12 cups
2 medium carrots, small julienne cut
In a large bowl toss it all up with 2t salt, let rest for an hour.
1 medium sweet onion, chopped

Dressing
1/2 cup homemade mayo with capers –if you can-
1/4 cup cider vinegar or to make it spicier combined it with Jalapeno pickle juice
1-2 T sugar
Salt and pepper to taste

Drain, squeezed out excess moisture from vegetables, add chopped onion and fold in dressing. This is one item you can guzzle down as much as you want; just take it easy on the ribs.

Spaghetti

I still remember the very first time I had the honor to taste this dish at one Italian Restaurant in Saigon City, 1969. The power of its flavor initially struck me like lightning, or I have to put it in another way: I was hooked at the first bite. I've cooked it enough through the years of raising kids and having fresh tomatoes from our own garden. The

process and essence of this dish change with the passage of time. Now it's just the two of us so making homemade sauce means lots of leftovers for the freezer. That's okay we'll live, because the commercial sauces that come out of the jar simply don't have the authority to bring me back to where it all began.

2t fennel seeds toasted and set aside.
2lbs hot Italian sausages
2lbs skirt steak cut into bite sized pieces
1cup chopped sweet onion
1 large bulb of garlic, peeled and crushed
1T dried hot pepper flakes
 1/4 cup tomatoes paste
1cup red wine
2 28 ounce cans diced tomatoes in juice
2-3 bay leaves
2t dried oregano
1t dried basil
Salt and pepper

In a Dutch pan with a light coat of olive oil, brown beef, remove to a bowl, do the same for sausages. Back to pan, sauté onion, garlic until fragrant stir in wine, tomato paste, followed by meat, sausages and the rest. Bring it all to boil, cover simmer for 1hr, and check for tenderness of meat. Meat should be tender but not falling apart in your mouth. Right here, your job is to adjust and balance out the seasoning to make it totally yours.

Lasagna

This item is featured regularly on the menu and it's totally different from one week to another. Early in May it might contain spinach, moving along to June the same project will change with Swiss chard or beet greens, and then the late summer brings zucchini or whatever I can salvage out of garden. But, it is always a vegetarian dish for a reason; that's how the fans like it.

The truly good lasagna doesn't need meat. Its entire stake is fresh vegetables, outstanding sauce with intense flavor, fresh herbs and a touch of gourmet cheese. I do this dish the way I see fit.

I always start it with generous sauce on the bottom; the next layer is no boil lasagna noodles (a blessed miracle of modern day technology to the culinary world). On top of that I'll put down a thick layer of sautéed vegetables, followed by ricotta cheese or tofu, another layer of vegetables then another round of noodles, sauce after that, and I seal it all with a thin layer of cheese, whatever kind that I have on hand. In this particular case, less is usually more, use quality gourmet cheese so you don't have to use a lot of it. The bottom line; have fun to create your own signature one.

When you do, the dish will speak for itself, period!

Apple pie

She busted into the middle school like a breath of fresh air, taking charge of the whole Girl Scout 'affairs. At that time our daughters were the same age and I was just one helping hand alongside a few other moms. I didn't know anything about her nor did anybody else, because she was a new kid in town but it was interesting how we became good friends.

I saw her husband in a dream, a tall slim man, dark hair and a nice smile. He introduced himself as her husband and asked me to bake an apple pie for her. I was arguing with the guy, giving him reasons why I didn't want to make a pie: too much work. I offered a stir fry instead. He insisted on apple pie because his wife doesn't like any spices at all, not even black pepper.

So at the end of the next Girl Scout meeting, I walked over and started a conversation with her. I came right to the point by introducing myself and stated that I saw her husband in my dream with his request. She seemed intrigued and not at all put off.

"What did he look like?' She asked, amused.

"Well, I couldn't really make out his face. I know for sure that he was tall, slim, dark hair with a friendly smile. Another thing he told me was that you don't like spices at all. What's up with that? Not even black pepper."

"Yeah, that's my Jim! He knows me so well'. There were sparkles of tears in her eyes.

"So why you giving me that weird look?" I said puzzled.

"He passed away. That's why we moved" then she smiled and her face light up. How can we not become friends? Clearly, I was handpicked just for her.

Fast forward later one afternoon while we were busy in her bakery kitchen, a business she was venturing. She stopped in the middle of scooping out cookie dough ice cream and gave me some information as I worked across the counter, making pie dough.

"I still don't understand why Jim asked you to bake an apple pie for me? Sorry, but they are not my favorite kind of pie"

"Don't you see that your husband knew you are going to buy this coffee shop long before you did and who would be suitable to be your wingman than a person with three apple pie blue ribbons under her belt," I shook my head.

"Did you really believe that?" She asks with a little awe in her voice.

"Yes I do, he knew you were going to do this."

Thanksgiving

I get asked often what kind of food usually gets served at my Thanksgiving table and they always seem disappointed when the answer is traditional.

I don't know why people dread overcooking a roasted dinner meal. I don't understand that. I'll show you my routine; effortlessly and seamlessly flow from beginning to end and the bonus of having the rest of that week free of cooking.

I do everything out of my head and never have to look up to any recipe from anybody. I haven't run into disaster yet and it's has been over thirty years.

Game plan on the day before: make the pie dough, chilled. Prep the bird.

Pie dough

2 sticks of butter cut into pea size, put in the freezer for 30 minutes

1//2 cup shortening – Forgive me, this is the only time out of the year I touch this stuff-

31/2 cup all purpose flour

2T sugar

2t salt

Iced water

In a large mixing bowl and a pastry blade, work the chilled butter into flour, salt, sugar and shortening together, you want a little bit of fat visible to the eyes, slowly pour in water, just enough until the dough is formed. Divide dough into three parts. Wrap and chill in refrigerator

Brine for the Turkey

7 quart of cold water

2 cups of gin

1/3 cup each of salt and sugar

Handful of crumb bay leaves

Handful of cracked pepper corn

This brine is good to a bird from 12 to 17lbs. I don't want it any bigger than that.

Submerge the bird into brine, store in refrigerator or a cold garage.

Prep for the appetizer- this item changes every year-

Make sure snack food such as nuts, candy, fruit, pickles, olives, cheese, crackers and drinks is ready.

The big day, the next day while everyone is still asleep, I go out to my kitchen and bake the pies, always two kinds: pumpkin pie and strawberry with rhubarb. Now you know why the dough is divided into three.

Pumpkin pie filling
2cups cooked pumpkin or 1 can
3/4 cup sugar
1/2t salt
1/4 cup molasses
2 large eggs
2t grated ginger
1t Saigon cinnamon
1/2t nutmeg
1T corn starch
Lemon juice (for a touch of tartness)
1 can of 12oz evaporated milk

In the oven heated to 400 degrees bake pie for 10 minutes, then lower heat to 350 and bake an extra 50 minutes more-or until set-

Strawberry pie
6 cups cut up strawberries
2 cups rhubarb cut up to ½ inches
1cup sugar
1/2t salt
11/2T each corn starch and tapioca starch

Bake it together in the same oven with the pumpkin pie.

Getting turkey ready for oven
Remove from brine; discard liquid, dry bird thoroughly
In the small bowl mix together 2t salt and 2t black pepper, rub spice in and out of cavity. I like the taste of lemon thyme and sage, so, a bundle of each will be used, last but not least garlic cloves, shallots tuck right in with herbs. Sew turkey up, brush with shallot oil. It's ready to go in the oven as soon as the pies are cooked.

Here's the time frame I'll use to get all my root vegetables cut up, set them aside; then turn around to make the dinner' rolls.

Yeast roll #1
>In a small bowl

2 packages of dry yeast
1cup warm water
1T each flour and sugar

>Set this aside to rest from 10 to 15 minutes
>When it all bubbles up in a large bowl or food processor with a dough hook, pour in:

1 1/2 cup warm water
2Tsugar
2t salt
2T vegetables oil

>Add yeast mixture into bowl and approximately 61/2 to 7 cups of flour, dough should be smooth and elastic. Roll it into a ball and cover it up inside of a large oiled bowl

Butter yeast rolls #2
2cups warm milk
2 eggs
1/4 cup sugar
1/3 cup melted butter
1t salt
2 package of dry yeast

>Mix well, add approximately 6 to 61/2 cups of all purpose or bread flour, knead dough for 10 minutes and turn it into a smooth ball, cover up and rest in a large oiled bowl.
>By now the pie is cooked; remove it from the oven, and replace it with the turkey.
>At this point I usually take a break to do my daily walk; it should take about 45 minutes.
>As soon as I get back, I start to work on the vegetables, steaming my best butter cup squash from our garden, making mash potatoes with roasted garlic, preparing little pearly white onions lazily laid in a luscious pool of butter and cream, peas, corn and one more dish of vegetables to play with. It could be asparagus or string beans; it's all depends on whose home for dinner. After all the vegetables are cooked, I put them in individual serving bowls, cover

them up. (When everything else is ready, all I have to do is run them through the microwave for a quick heat up).

By then the dough should be ready to punch down, divide yeast roll #1 into 12 balls set them in a large baking pan and let them rise until they double in size. This is the bread that will be used for sandwiches later.

Dough #2 is intended for dinner. Punch it down, and divide it into 16 pieces, this particular dough is extremely easy to work with, so, sometimes it can be crescent or clover' shaped or whatever I'm in the mood for. At this point, the turkey is ready to come out of the oven to be replaced with the rolls. Raise oven temperature to 400 degree, it takes 20 minutes for bread and 15 minutes for butter roll.

Making the gravy

This is the last chore, after removing the turkey; transfer the bird to a serving plate. Tips for smoother gravy: for every cup of liquid I would use the mixture of one each teaspoon of corn starch, potato starch and tapioca. Always use broth mixed in with that gooey brown from the bottom of pan. Fresh herbs may be used on top gravy to entertain your eyes.

We usually eat the same dinner Friday night. After that, I would lay the rest of mash potatoes down (the size of pan depends on how much left over I have) layer the rest of whatever vegetables available at the time, cut up turkey, gravy, cheese and on top sprinkle in more black pepper with a hand full of crispy shallots. Wrap it up in foil; by Sunday night put it in 350 degree oven for 45 minutes. There's your day off!

What about Saturday? This is the day you should be eating very lightly to show a little respect toward your body since (if you do what I did) the damage has already been done for two days in a row. So, a salad and a roll would be perfect!

Our Bodyguard

Soonie was a full grown dog when he entered our lives. He didn't have a very good life before that, he got beat up frequently because the previous owner was very cruel to him. So, for a longest time he was actually frightened when we would shower him with affection.

This dog was coming into my life as the result of a conspiracy between my daughter Samantha and her dad. They knew I had no desire for a large dog so, for the most part, they worked out a plan then brought him home. Of course I put up a fight and stood up to my code: no big dogs! Steve said we've got him for now so let's show him around. He and Sam took Soonie down to the basement and wouldn't you know at that instant a ground squirrel chewed through the dryer vent. Soonie caught it and he turned and handed me his prize. I always say he bribed his way into my existence.

Every morning we would go for a walk, Soonie and I, and he would always walk side by side with me. I never had to put a leash on him. I have been walking along side that same road for what seems to be hundred years yet nobody noticed me until Soonie tagged along.

Time and time again I would run into a stranger and they would praise what a beautiful and well behaved dog he was. Many people began recognizing me as the lady who walked with the black lab.

"Yes, he's my body guard, so, don't mess with me" I often responded.

The person Soonie preferred to following around would be his master, second choice definitely my daughter Samantha. But, when neither of his two favorites was available, he'd settle for me. In the garden, outside my kitchen' door, or waiting patiently for the next treat, I like to think he just wanted to hang around with me.

Soonie pulled double duty, walking with me in the morning, same thing in the evening with my husband and the two of them frequently went snow-shoeing all winter long.

One late afternoon they went for a walk, it was in the early winter, so it was getting dark rather quickly, I waited and waited then finally they walked through the door and facing me, with my motor mouth running I yelled, "Where did you two go for a walk, China?"

My husband's voice was rather weary.

"I slipped and hit my head and must have fallen in the ditch and blacked out, because when I regained conscious and opened my eyes all I could see was the bright moon over Soonie, his body right on top of my chest, I don't know how long he was guarding me."

Well, let me share a bit of information about the man I married. Over thirty years I've known him to damage many parts of his body. He has fallen down in the middle of the day before due to a concussion and has had cuts and bruises that he couldn't recall how they got there; I say he's got elephant skin. But still, it terrified me just the same. As far as he was concerned this was just another minor incident but the fact that Soonie laid on him and kept him warm made his dog a HERO.

We didn't know how old Soonie was when he came into our lives, but we made sure he had a good life; we were making up for the hardship he dealt with before that.

Along down the road one day, I realized he was not enjoying the walks anymore so I let my dog off the hook and started going solo once again. That's when cars stopped on occasion and caring people with questions asked regarding his whereabouts, my answer was the same, "My body guard is retired"

At almost the end, we recognized his health was slipping, but, neither of us ever dared to verbalize what was on our mind. It hurt me, but even more so for my husband, that our boy was an old man and he was no longer having fun. I couldn't even talk about it much less take any action.

One summer day I was getting ready to go gather supplies for the week ahead and my husband said to me in a somewhat casual fashion pointing at Soonie who lay nearby,

"Why don't you give him an extra hug and say goodbye, after all, you are going to be away almost all day."

I was in a hurry, of course I always am in a rush, that's one of my flaws (out of thousands)which is why I didn't see it coming. I sped over giving Soonie a quick hug; then dashing out of the door, I didn't realize that's was the last time I was able to touch my boy.

That particular day as I vividly recall, I didn't feel very well. Not in the sense of physically, just the dreadful feeling, and I failed to pinpoint what was wrong with me.

About midday, there was a sharp pain piercing through the cavity of my chest while I was driving, I had to pull the car over and recollect myself. The pain went away, but, the awful feeling remained.

When I was walking into the garage that late afternoon, I didn't see my dog; his usual greeting was not in place. I saw my husband, one look into his face: I just knew.

I had seen that impression before, the torn face, the red swollen eyes when he had to put our Australian terrier to sleep years ago. Finally he found his cracked voice,

"I know you have to do all that running around, so, I couldn't tell you..."

I asked him about what the time was when he had his last moments with Soonie which clearly I already knew. Exactly what I thought, all that explained the moment I was in twilight zone earlier.

I can't really say I was surprised, he had a good plan to bring Soonie into our home and he had a good plan to bring his boy to his final rest: I don't envy his mission.

"Where is he?" I asked as we were embraced each other.

"I already buried him" He said, his voice unstable. With this information, I know exactly where he was, up on the hill next to Ben our first dog and Mia our one and only cat.

"I have been working on his casket recently," he explained. Knowing his work ethic the box must be evenly square every angle and fit our boy to the T.

If only I'm not so wrapped up in what I do, I should have suspected all this was coming. All and all he was the one taking on the burden of the whole operation.

It was difficult breathing as I neared where Soonie lay; I stared down at the newly dug dirt. A sob escaped me and I kneeled down to touch the ground that swallowed my boy. Tears flowed as I choked between my words saying good- bye to him. The next sentence comes from deep in my heart.

I love my dog and I can't fathom the fact that I didn't even want him at first.

She's back

The summer of 2009 began with an historic numbers of days of miserable soaking rain, weekdays and weekends. The first sunny and warm Sunday in Bar Harbor had all the people out, the lines were long at my table and Sam wasn't with me that particular weekend. She'd traveled with her two sisters to visit my family in Washington, DC.

As I was happily packaging his order, the customer said,

"Please, you have to separate this order into two bags."

"Of course, I can do that."

Then he went on and explained the reason,

"A friend of mine loves your food and he hasn't had any of it since his wife passed away. I just happened to be in town so I thought it would be nice to surprise him with a package from you"

"That's very thoughtful of you!" I said it with a sincere smile.

While talking to him my eyes were traveling through the line in the front of me, suddenly I spotted the "That's enough lady" half way through the crowd, immediately I think of Sam, and I secretly smile at the thought I'd beat her at her own game this time (You might want to go back and look at the other half of this story with the title "THE THAT'S ENOUGH LADY" to make sense out of what I'm saying right now.

She waves at me with both of her hands and a beaming smile; I think this is strange because she's never done that before and I noticed she not wearing her usual red glasses and the cane is gone.

The customer's words bring me back to face him,

"You might remember her. He said she's about this tall, using his hand, wears red glasses and she usually walks with a cane, she died…"

"Two years ago this summer."

"Yes, you do remember Mrs. William," he exclaimed.

I do now.

I don't have to look up to know she's not there anymore, in the middle of August heat I felt a shiver run up and down my neck, my hands shake as I reached out to his,

"I really appreciate you coming here today, sir. Please, tell him I'm sorry for his loss, she was a good customer. We've wondered for a while what might've happened.'

I almost wanted to add

"By the way, she doesn't have to wear glasses or need her cane anymore". But I didn't. At the time it was just a private thing between Mrs. William and me. After all she was the one who granted me my wish that I can serve her one more time.

For the rest of that day, I walked around with a grin on my face and a very warm feeling inside my chest. You should've seen Samantha eyes pop open when I told her how Mrs. William let me beat her out of that game for the very last time!

Last Thoughts

There you have it, my second book. I would like to thank each and every one of you who've read my first one and encouraged me to work to do another. Life always takes some strange turns. All my life I never dreamed of becoming a writer, much less the kind of writer who savors every minute of the process. How crazy is it? I made myself laugh and at the same time I can't stop the erosion of sadness when I talk about the customers who passed away.

Some day, when it's all said and done, I would like to thank you for the beautiful memories all of you have given me at the market. That's something nobody can take away from me. It's my special keepsake. I hope you'll always treat yourself, and your family to healthy meals and I hope you will continue to visit your local farmer's market.

Last, but not least: think and pray for the safe return of our men and women who are fighting for our freedom. Freedom isn't free; remember they are the ones missing at their own dinner's table tonight.

Sincerely,
Bich Nga

Recipes Index

Soup
Hot and sour-12
Egg drop-13
Asparagus with Crab meat-13
Miso with Tofu and Greens-15
Hot and sour Shrimp with Fiddle
    head-16

Small Bites
Happy Dumplings-17
Dumpling with Tofu and
    Spinach-19
Shrimp Toast-22
Steamed Bun with Pork, chicken
    and Shiitake mushroom-24
Stuffed Grape leaves with Beef-26
Beef in Orange sauce with
    Cashew-27

Bird of all season
Mainely Chicken-31
Chicken with Ginger and Saffron-32
General's Nga Chicken-33
(Oven) Fried chicken-35
Sweet and spicy Chicken-37
Emma's Roasted Chicken with
    Lemongrass-38
Roasted Chicken w/ Five
    Fragrance-39
Special Duck-41
Chicken with Rosemary, Cherry
    Tomatoes and Black Olive-43

From the sea
Steamed Crab Cake-46
Fish stew with Tomatoes
    and Herbs-49
Lazy day Fish-50
Braised Fish with Eggplant,
    Tomatoes and Herbs-50
Roasted Salmon with Wilted
    Green-51
Creamy Scallops with Yellow
    curry-52
Fish steak in Tomatoes and Dill
    sauce-53
Beautiful Flounder-54
Skinny Shrimp-54
Yard long Bean and Shrimp-55
Happy Shrimp in creamy Tofu
    sauce-56

For the Love of Pork
Eggplant and spicy Pork-60
Survivor Pork-61
Tenderloin Pork with Grape
    Tomatoes-63
Luscious Chops in Black Bean
    sauce- 64
A Pate for all Occasion-65
Bird Nest Pate and Egg-66
The Found Meat Balls-67
Sweet and Succulent Spare Ribs
    Nuggets-69

For the Love of Ribs and Honey-70
Funny Pork with Tequila and Lime
    juice-71
Stuffed Tomatoes with Pork-73
Stuffed Cabbages with Chicken
    and Pork-74
Stuffed sweet Onion with Spicy
    Pork-75

Tofu
Golden Lady-78
Lady and the golden Beets-79
Lady in Red-80
Lady in Yellow Curry sauce-82
Lady in Green-83
Tofu Swish Chard and Shiitake
    Mushroom-84
Lady in the Black Forest-86
Lady in the Golden Pond-87
Rich man's Lady-88
Lady under the Rainbow-89
Sophisticated Lady-90
Lady in Good company-91
Stuffy Lady- 92

Rice and Noodles
Brown rice-95
Jasmine-95
Special Day Fried rice-95
Vegetables Fried rice-96
Red rice-96
Green rice-97
Green rice with a kick-98
Sunday Noodles and Shrimp with
    Coconut-99
Kay's Rice Noodles-102
Baby Love Rice Noodles with tofu
    and Bean Sprout-103

The Special of Everyday Vegetables
Asparagus with Crab Meat and
    Ground Pork-106

Broccoli-106
Bok choy-107
A wild green meet Beef-107
Napa Cabbagge-108
Spring Bean-108
Tossed String Bean with
    Sesame Ginger-109
Corn with Coconut Cream-109
Wheat free Tempura Vegetables-110
Swiss Chard-110
Cauliflower-111
Eggplant-111
Potatoes Patties-112
The many faces of Kale-113
Twenty minutes Kidney Beans-114
Back Bean Patties-115
Marinated Chickpeas-116
Red Beans and Greens-117

Salad for all season
Cucmber-118
Sweet Spicy Petite Cucumber-119
Cucumber with Herbs and
    Nuts-119
Sweet Potatoes in Salad-119
String Beans in Salad- 120
Kohlrabi in Salad-121
Zucchini in Salad-122
Red Lentil in Salad-123
Black Bean and Corn in Salad-123
Pineapple in Salad-124
Shrimp and Avocado Salad-126
Sarah's Shrimp Salad-127
Chicken Salad-128
Poached Chicken Salad with
    shredded Cabbages-129
Chicken Salad and Avocado in
    Tequila Dressing-131
Quick pan seared Chicken with
    Sugar Pea Salad-132

Summer fare
The salt Factor in Rubs-134
Junne Fire Grill Beef-136
A few Steak dinners for my Dad-138
Spicy Grill Beef with
     Lemongrass-139
The Bad Boy- T bone Steak-140
Grilled Steak in Ginger and Wine
     Dressing-141
Sate for the Grill-142
Great Corn inside the Husk-145

Sweet Treats
Creamy Coconut Custard and
     Ginger Caramel over Delicata
     Squash-147
Creamy Silken Tofu in Ginger
     syrup-150
Tropical Fruit Salad for Dessert-151
Berries Beauty-152
Sunshine Mango Custard with
     Gorgeous Raspberry sauce-152

Fried Banana for Dessert-153
Banana with Tapioca Pearl and
     Coconut-154
Sweet Potatoes with Cassava
     Root-156

White People Food
Meat ball for other occasions-158
Mac and Cheese-159
B.B.Q. Ribs-160
Coleslaw-161
Spaghetti-162
Lasagna-162
Pie dough-164
Brined for Turkey-164
Pumpkin Pie-165
Strawberry Pie-165
Yeast Rolls#1-166
Butter rolls#2-166

Short Story Index

Spring Feast-10
The pink Diamond-12
The power of a sincere
    Thank You Note-14
For the Love of Dumplings-17
Sister Tien-19
The Sandwich Diet-23
The stud muffin from
    Stonington-29
The wise man-30
My Diet Ordeal-31
The Famous Chicken-33
The Devoted Customer-34
That's enough!-36
Emma-38
Jenny-38
Angel on Fire-40
Market Fun day-42
The Hopeful one-44
Yvonne and her Fine Catch-46
The Old Fashion Way-47
The Advice-49
The Happy Diamond-56
The Tale of an Apprentice
    and her Sensei-58
Pork Eggplant and Lily-58
Say Hello to your new
    Best Friend-61
The Mistake-62
The other Stud Muffin from
    Stonington-64

The lost Meat Balls-66
The Zero Heroes-68
The Love from Bar Harbor-69
The Comedian-71
The Secret Affair-72
The Last Sunday-77
The Rose Effect-79
My Fifty Cents Sale-81
Festival Kale-82
Sunset Sweet Diamond-83
The Busy Summer's Day of
    Bar Harbor-85
Paula's Bad Week-90
The Gnome from Belfast-91
The Number According to
    Samantha-94
An Afternoon with the Lady-98
My Twin Kay: The Bonus-101
The Leaf is Beautiful!-105
Mayonnaise without End-118
Appleton Creamery-121
Black Bean and Corn-123
Stanley and his Lovely wife-125
Lena and the Avocado Salad-130
I Like Women!-135
Sleeping with the Enemy-135
Farewell to my Father-137
My Famous "Neighbor"-141
Baby in the Corn Husk-143
The out of Town-147
Happy Food-148

Pudding in the Rain-154
Claudia-115
Apple Pie-163
Our Body Guard-167
She's Back-170

CPSIA information can be obtained at www.ICGtesting.com
Printed in the USA
LVOW112058201011

251456LV00004B/4/P